P9-DEL-592

Flowers that are mostly blue .... pg. 3-57

Flowers that are mostly brown .... pg. 59-61

Flowers that are mostly green .... pg. 63-77

Flowers that are mostly orange .... pg. 79-89

Flowers that have prominent pink .... pg. 91-121

Flowers that are mostly purple .... pg. 123-155

Flowers that are mostly red .... pg. 157-175

Flowers that are mostly white .... pg. 177-311

Flowers that are mostly yellow .... pg. 313-401

Wildflowers

of

Minnesota

Field Guide

by Stan Tekiela

**ADVENTURE PUBLICATIONS, INC.
CAMBRIDGE, MINNESOTA**

To my daughter, Abigail Rose: The sweetest flower in my life.

ACKNOWLEDGMENTS

I would like to thank Kathy Heidel, a very special naturalist with extraordinary knowledge of the wildflowers of Minnesota. I will always have a special place in my heart for her. And thanks to John D. Jackson, Ph.D., a botanist, who continues to guide me through the wonderful world of wildflowers.

Book and icon design by Jonathan Norberg

Photo credits:
Cover photo: Showy Lady's Slipper by Stan Tekiela
Dudley Edmondson: 2, 4, 8, 14, 16, 18, 20, 22, 24, 24 (flower), 28, 30, 38, 44, 46, 48, 50, 52 (field), 56, 58, 62, 64, 68, 70, 74, 76, 78, 80, 82, 84, 90, 96, 98, 100, 106, 110, 116, 118, 120, 126, 134, 136, 140, 148, 152, 154, 156, 158, 160, 162, 164, 166, 168, 170, 170 (flower), 172, 174, 176, 180, 182 (fruit), 184, 186, 192, 196, 198, 202, 204, 206, 210, 212, 216, 218, 220, 224, 226, 228, 230, 232, 234, 236, 238, 244, 250, 254, 256, 260, 266, 268, 276, 278, 280, 282, 286, 288, 292, 294, 308, 312, 314, 318, 320, 324, 326, 328, 334, 340, 344, 350, 354, 356, 358, 362, 368, 370, 376, 380, 384, 388, 392, 394, 398, 400
David Fennell: 156 (seed) **Richard Haug:** 102, 114, 178, 206 (fruit), 242 **Steve Mortenson:** 130, 166 (fruit), 178 (fruit), 182, 190, 212 (fruit), 236 (fruit) **John Pennoyer:** 208 **Stan Tekiela:** 6, 10, 12, 26, 32, 34, 36, 40, 42, 52 (flower), 54, 60, 66 (both), 72 (both), 74 (fruit), 84 (fruit), 86, 88, 92 (fruit), 94, 104, 106 (fruit), 108, 122 (both), 124, 128, 132, 138, 142, 144, 146, 150, 172 (fruit), 188, 194 (both), 200, 214, 222, 240, 240 (fruit), 246, 248, 252, 258 (both), 262, 262 (fruit), 264, 264 (fruit), 270, 272, 274, 284, 290, 296 (both), 298, 300, 302, 302 (fruit), 304, 306, 310, 316, 322, 330, 332, 336, 338, 342, 346, 348, 352, 360, 364, 366 (both), 372, 374, 378, 382, 386, 390, 396 (both) **Larry Weber:** 92, 112

10 9 8 7
Copyright 1999 by Stan Tekiela
Published by Adventure Publications, Inc.
820 Cleveland St. S
Cambridge, MN 55008
1-800-678-7006
www.adventurepublications.net

ISBN-13: 978-1-885061-63-8
ISBN-10: 1-885061-63-3

TABLE OF CONTENTS

Introduction iv

The Wildflowers...1

    Blue 3

    Brown...59

    Green 63

    Orange 79

    Pink 91

    Purple...123

    Red 157

    White 177

    Yellow...313

Check List/Index 402

Glossary 406

MINNESOTA AND WILDFLOWERS

Minnesota is a great place for wildflower enthusiasts! Our state is at the crossroads of three major vegetative habitats. Each of these vegetative zones contains a wide and often unique variety of wildflowers. Our upper-Midwest location is unique because we have a western wildflower influence, an even stronger eastern influence and a strong northern boreal influence. All of this means Minnesota is fortunate to have an extremely diverse, often unique and certainly a very healthy variety of wonderful wildflowers.

The Wildflowers of Minnesota Field Guide is an easy-to-use field guide to help the curious nature seeker identify 200 of the most common wildflowers in Minnesota. It features, with only a few exceptions, the herbaceous wildflowers of Minnesota. Herbaceous plants have soft green stems and die back to the ground each fall. Only a few plants with woody stems have been included because these particular plants are very common and have large showy flowers.

STRATEGIES FOR IDENTIFYING WILDFLOWERS

Determining the color of the flower is the first step in a simple five-step process to identify a wildflower.

Because this guide is organized by color, identifying an unknown wildflower is as simple as matching the color of the flower to the color section of the book. The color tabs on each page identify the color section.

The second step in determining the identity of a wildflower is the size. Within each color section, the flowers are arranged by the size of the flower, or flower cluster, from small to large. A plant with a single, small, yellow flower will be in the beginning of the yellow section while a large white flower will be towards the end of the white section. Sometimes flowers are made up of many individual flowers in clusters that are perceived to be one larger flower. Therefore, these will be ordered by the size of the cluster, not the individual flower. See page 410 for rulers to help estimate flower and leaf size.

Once you have determined the color and approximate size, observe the appearance of the flower. Is it a single flower or cluster of flowers? If it is a cluster, is the general shape of the cluster flat, round or spike? For the single flowers, note if the flower has a regular, irregular, bell or tube shape. Also, counting the number of petals might help to identify these individual flowers. Compare your findings with the descriptions on each page. Examining the flower as described above should result in narrowing the identity of the wildflower down to just a few candidates.

The fourth step is to look at the leaves. There are several possible shapes or types of leaves. Simple leaves have only one leaf blade but can be lobed. Compound leaves have a long central leaf stalk with many smaller leaflets attached. Twice compound leaves have two or more leaf stalks and many leaflets. Sometimes it is helpful to note if the leaves have toothed or smooth margins (edges), so look for this also.

For the fifth step, check to see how the leaf is attached to the stem. Some plants may look similar but have different leaf attachments so this can be very helpful. Look to see if the leaves are attached opposite of each other along the stem, alternately, or whorled around a point on the stem. Sometimes the leaves occur at the base of the plant (basal). Some leaves do not have a leaf stalk and clasp the stem at their base (clasping) and in some cases the stem appears to pass through the base of the leaf (perfoliate).

Using these five steps (color, size, shape, leaves and leaf attachment) will help you gather the clues needed to quickly and easily identify the common wildflowers of Minnesota.

USING THE ICONS

Sometimes the botanical terms for leaf type, attachment and type of flower can be confusing and difficult to remember. Because of this, we have included icons at the bottom of each page. They can be used to quickly and visually match the main features of the plant to the specimen you are viewing without even needing to completely understand the botanical terms. By using the photos, text descriptions and icons in this field guide, you should be able to quickly and easily identify most of the common wildflowers of Minnesota.

The icons are arranged from left to right in the following order: flower cluster type, flower type, leaf type, leaf attachment and fruit. The first two flower icons refer to cluster type and flower type. While these are not botanically separate categories, we have made separate icons for them to simplify identification.

FLOWER CLUSTER ICONS

     (icon color is dependent on flower color)

Flat   **Round**   **Spike**

Any cluster (tightly formed group) of flowers can be categorized into one of three cluster types based on its over-all shape. The flat, round and spike types refer to the cluster shape which is easy to observe. Technically there is another cluster type, composite, which appears as a single daisy-like flower but is actually a cluster of many tiny flowers. Because this is often perceived as a flower type, we have included the icon in the flower type section. See page viii for its description.

Some examples of cluster types

Flat   Round   Spike

FLOWER TYPE ICONS

     (icon color is dependent on flower color)

Regular **Irregular** **Composite** **Bell** **Tube**

Botanically speaking, there are many types of flowers but in this guide, we are simplifying them to five basic types. Regular flowers are defined as having a round shape with three or more petals, lacking a disk-like center. Irregular flowers are not round but uniquely-shaped with fused petals. Bell flowers are hanging with fused petals. Tube flowers are longer and narrower than bell flowers and point up. Composite flowers (technically a flower cluster) are usually round compact clusters of tiny flowers appearing as one larger flower.

Some examples of flower types

Regular   Irregular   Bell

disk flowers
ray flowers

Tube   Composite

Composite cluster: Although a composite flower is technically a type of flower cluster, we are including the icon in the flower type category since most people not familiar with botany would visually see it as a flower type, not a flower cluster. A composite flower consists of petals (ray flowers) and/or a round disk-like center (disk flowers). Sometimes a flower has only ray flowers, sometimes only disk flowers or both.

LEAF TYPE ICONS

Simple

Simple
Lobed

Compound

Twice
Compound

Palmate

Leaf type can be broken down into two main types; simple and compound. Simple leaves are leaves that are in one piece; the leaf is not divided into smaller leaflets. It can have teeth or be smooth along the edges. The simple leaf is depicted by the simple leaf icon. Simple leaves may have lobes and sinuses that give the leaf a unique shape. These simple leaves with lobes are depicted by the simple lobed icon.

Some examples of leaf types

Simple

Simple Lobed

Compound

Twice Compound

Palmate

Compound leaves have two or more distinct, small leaves called leaflets that arise from a single stalk. In this field guide we are dividing compound leaves into regular compound, twice compound or palmately compound leaves. Twice compound leaves are those that have many distinct leaflets arising from a secondary leaf stalk. Palmately compound leaves are those with three or more leaflets arising from a common central point.

LEAF ATTACHMENT ICONS

Alternate   **Basal**   **Clasping**   **Opposite**   **Perfoliate**   **Whorl**

Leaves attach to the stems in different ways for different plants. Check to see where and how each leaf is attached to the main stem. There are six main types of attachment as indicated but sometimes, a plant can have two different types of attachments. This is most often seen in the combination of basal leaves and leaves that attach along the main stem either alternate or opposite (cauline leaves). These wildflowers have some leaves at the base of the plant, usually in a rosette pattern, and some leaves along the stem. In these cases, both icons are presented but for most plants, there will only be one leaf attachment icon.

Some examples of leaf attachment

Alternate   Opposite   Whorl

Perfoliate   Clasping   Basal

Alternate leaves attach to the stem in an alternating pattern while opposite leaves attach to the stem directly opposite from each other. Whorled leaves have three or more leaves that attach around the stem at the same point. Clasping leaves have no stalk and the base of the leaf partly surrounds the main stem. Perfoliate leaves are also stalkless and have a leaf base that completely surrounds the main stem. Basal leaves are those that originate at the base of a plant, near the ground, usually grouped in a round rosette.

FRUIT ICONS

Berry **Pod**

(icon color is dependent on fruit color)

In some flower descriptions a fruit category has been included. This may be especially useful when a plant is not in bloom or when the fruit is particularly large or otherwise noteworthy. Botanically speaking, there are many types of fruit. We have simplified these often confusing fruit categories into two general groups, berry and pod.

Some examples of fruit types

Berry   Pod

The berry icon is used to depict a soft, fleshy, often round structure containing seeds. The pod icon is used to represent a dry structure that, when mature, splits open to release seeds.

SEASON OF BLOOM

Most wildflowers have a specific season of blooming. For example, you probably won't see the common spring-blooming Yellow Trout Lily blooming in summer or fall. Knowing the season of bloom can help you narrow your selection as you try to identify an unknown flower. In this field guide, spring usually means April, May and the first half of June. Summer refers to the last half of June, July and August. Fall usually means September and October.

LIFE CYCLE/ORIGIN

The life cycle of a wildflower describes how long a wildflower lives. Annual wildflowers are short-lived. They sprout, grow and bloom in only one season, never to return except from seed. Most wildflowers .have perennial life cycles that last may years. Perennial wildflowers are usually deeply-rooted plants that grow from the roots each year. They return each year from their roots but they also produce seeds to start other perennial plants. Similar to the annual life cycle is the biennial cycle. This group of plants takes two seasons of growth to bloom. The first year the plant produces a low growth of basal leaves. During the second year, the plant sends up a flower stalk from which it produces seeds, from which new plants can be started. However, the original plant will not return for a third year of growth.

Origin indicates whether the plants are native or non-native. Most of the wildflowers in this book originate in Minnesota and are considered native plants. Non-native plants were often unintentionally introduced when they escaped from gardens or farms. Most non-native plants are now naturalized in Minnesota.

HABITATS

Some wildflowers thrive only in specific habitats. They may require certain types of soil, moisture, pH levels, fungi or nutrients. Other wildflowers are generalists and can grow just about anywhere. Sometimes noting the habitat surrounding the flower in question can be a clue to its identity.

RANGE

The wide variety of habitats in Minnesota naturally restricts the range of certain wildflowers that have specific requirements. For example, a wildflower such as Pearly Everlasting that requires dry acid soils may only be found in northeastern Minnesota. Sometimes this section can help you eliminate a wildflower from consideration just based on its range. However, please keep in mind that the ranges indicated are general notations on where the flower is commonly found. They are general guidelines only and there will certainly be exceptions to these ranges.

STAN'S NOTES

Stan's Notes is fun and fact-filled with many interesting "gee-whiz" tidbits of information such as historical uses, other common names, insect relationship, color variations and much more. Much of the information in this section cannot be found in other wildflower field guides.

BOUNDARY WATERS CANOE AREA/ NATIVE PRAIRIE PLANTS

Near the page number on many of the wildflowers, you will notice a canoe or bunch of grass. These icons will help you quickly identify which wildflowers are common to the Boundary Waters Canoe Area and which inhabit one of Minnesota's rarest of habitat, the native prairie. A lack of such a symbol does not mean you absolutely won't find these plants in these areas, it just means they aren't commonly seen there. These are indicated because many people travel to canoe the BWCA wilderness and this guide will help to identify the wildflowers there. And, more and more people are becoming interested in native prairies and their value to our ecosystem. Many people travel to the remaining native prairies and this will guide will help to identify the wildflowers that grow in these habitats.

CAUTION

A word of caution. In Stan's Notes, it is mentioned that in some cultures, some of the wildflowers were used for medicine or food. While some find this interesting, DO NOT use this guide to identify edible or medicinal plants. Some of the wildflowers in Minnesota are toxic or have toxic look-alikes that can cause severe problems. Do not take the chance of making a mistake. Please enjoy the wildflowers with your eyes, nose or with your camera. In addition, please don't pick, trample or transplant any of the wildflowers you see. The flower of a plant is its reproductive structure and if you pick a flower you have eliminated its ability to reproduce itself. Transplanting wildflowers is another destructive occurrence. Most wildflowers need specific soil types, pH levels or special bacteria or fungi in the soil to grow properly. If you try to transplant a wildflower to a habitat not suitable for its particular needs, the wildflower most likely will die. Many of our Minnesota wildflowers are now available from your local garden centers. These wildflowers have been cultivated and have not been dug from the wild.

Enjoy the Wild Wildflowers!

Stan

COMMON NAME
Scientific name

Family: plant family name

COLOR INDICATOR

Height: height of plant

Flower: general description, type of flower, size of flower, number of petals

Leaf: general description, size, leaf type, type of attachment, toothed or smooth

Fruit: berry or pod

Bloom: spring, summer, fall

Cycle/Origin: annual, perennial, biennial, native, non-native

Habitat: general environment in which you are likely to find the flower

Range: throughout or part of the state flower is found

Stan's Notes: helpful identification information, history, origin and other interesting, "gee-whiz" nature facts

Not all icons are found on every page. See preceeding pages for icon descriptions.

Some pages have one of these icons indicating the flower is prevalent in the BWCA or native prairies.

CLUSTER TYPE	FLOWER TYPE	LEAF TYPE	LEAF ATTACHMENT	FRUIT
Spike	**Regular**	**Simple**	**Alternate**	**Berry**

FORGET-ME-NOT
Myosotis scorpioides

Family: Borage (Boraginaceae)

Height: 6-12" (15-30 cm)

Flower: a fusion of 5 petals forms tiny baby blue flowers with yellow centers (eye); each flower, ¼" (.6 cm) wide, sits atop 2 uncoiling stems; stems are curled and unfurl when the flowers begin to bloom

Leaf: blunt, lance-shaped stemless leaves, 1-2" (2.5-5 cm) long, alternate along the stem; each leaf is covered in fine hair

Bloom: spring, summer, fall

Cycle/Origin: perennial, non-native

Habitat: wet, shade, along streams, rivers and creeks

Range: locally around cities and homes

Stan's Notes: Also called True Forget-me-not, this Eurasian import has escaped gardens and grows along Minnesota's rivers and streams. It can live directly in water but is usually found in moist soil, growing in large mats along an extensive fibrous root system. Four species of Forget-me-not are found in Minnesota, some native. Another old name for this plant, Scorpion Weed, refers to its coiled flower stalk, which resembles the coiled tail of a scorpion. Some suggest that the common name comes from the plant's unpleasant taste or odor that is hard to forget. Another story is about a suitor who reached too far over a cliff to obtain the flower for his love, fell and cried out, "Forget me not!"

FLOWER TYPE	LEAF TYPE	LEAF ATTACHMENT
		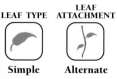
Regular	Simple	Alternate

GROUND IVY
Glechoma hederacea

Family: Mint (Lamiaceae)

Height: 5-8" (12.5-20 cm)

Flower: light blue-to-purple flowers, ¼-¾" (.6-2 cm) long; 2-4 flowers on short stalks that arise at a leaf joint; 5 petals fuse to form a flower

Leaf: round, sometimes kidney-shaped leaves, ½-1½" (1-4 cm) wide, with deep veins and coarse scalloped teeth along the edge; often purplish in color with a wavy edge

Bloom: spring, summer

Cycle/Origin: perennial, non-native

Habitat: dry, shade, disturbed soil and especially lawns

Range: throughout

Stan's Notes: This is not an ivy but a Eurasian import of the Mint family. It is highly scented and can be identified simply by crushing and smelling it. Like all mints, its stem is square and it has opposite leaves. It roots to the ground at each leaf attachment (node), allowing the plant to "creep" across the ground (hence one of its common names, Creeping Charley). Another common name, Gill-over-the-ground, comes from the French *guiller* (to ferment), because its leaves were once used to ferment and flavor beer. It grows in large carpets in moist semi-shaded areas and is considered a weed because of its aggressive growing nature.

FLOWER TYPE	LEAF TYPE	LEAF ATTACHMENT
Irregular	**Simple**	**Opposite**

ASIATIC DAYFLOWER
Commelina communis

Family: Spiderwort (Commelinaceae)

Height: 1-3' (30-90 cm)

Flower: usually only one blue and white flower, ¾" (2 cm) wide, located at the tip of each stem; flower has 3 petals, 2 upper blue and 1 lower white

Leaf: toothless, stalkless, lance-shaped leaves, 3-5" (7.5-12.5 cm) long, attach directly to the stem, with the leaf base folding around the stem at the point of attachment; leaves nearest the flowers are much smaller and nearly heart-shaped, sometimes cradling the flower

Bloom: spring, summer, fall

Growth: annual, non-native

Habitat: moist, disturbed areas, roadsides, gardens

Range: in and around large metropolitan areas of the state

Stan's Notes: As its name suggests, the Asiatic Dayflower, essentially a garden weed, was introduced from Asia. It is usually found only in metro areas because it most often reaches gardens from purchased bags of soil. Flowers bloom only for one day, hence the common name, "Dayflower." Its species name, *communis*, refers to the colonies it forms by rooting from each stem node (where each leaf attaches). Several similar species are also found in Minnesota. This is a host plant for Pearl Crescent butterfly caterpillars.

FLOWER TYPE	LEAF TYPE	LEAF ATTACHMENT	LEAF ATTACHMENT
Irregular	Simple	Alternate	Clasping

BLUE-EYED GRASS
Sisyrinchium montanum

Family: Iris (Iridaceae)

Height: 4-20" (10-50 cm)

Flower: a collection of tiny blue flowers with a bright yellow center, individual flowers, ½" (1 cm) wide, have 6 petals, each tipped with a small point; each flower group rises from a short stalk, which in turn comes from a longer leaflike stem

Leaf: thin, pointed, grass-like leaves, ¼" (.6 cm) wide, up to 2" (5 cm) long, that are often confused with blades of grass

Fruit: a round pod

Bloom: spring, summer

Cycle/Origin: perennial, native

Habitat: wet, meadows, roadsides, prairies

Range: throughout

Stan's Notes: Often confused with a type of grass, Blue-eyed Grass is actually a member of the Iris family. The most common of several species in Minnesota and one of over 40 species in North America, Blue-eyed Grass has fibrous vertical roots, unlike the more common irises, which spread on a horizontal rhizome. Like other irises, Blue-eyed Grass is made up of three sepals (leaves that look like petals) and three petals. Each petal is shallowly notched with tiny tips. Stems can sometimes be bluish purple.

FLOWER TYPE	LEAF TYPE	LEAF ATTACHMENT	FRUIT
Regular	**Simple**	**Basal**	**Pod**

9

ROUND-LOBED HEPATICA
Hepatica americana

Family: Buttercup (Ranunculaceae)

Height: 4-6" (10-15 cm)

Flower: flowers have 5-9 petal-like sepals that range in color from pale blue to lavender, pink and white, and have 3 green bracts underneath; each flower, ½-1" (1-2.5 cm) wide, sits on a single hairy stalk and sometimes droops downward

Leaf: each basal leaf has 3 round lobes rising from a thin hairy stalk

Bloom: spring

Cycle/Origin: perennial, native

Habitat: dry, shade, deciduous woods

Range: throughout, but more common in the northern half

Stan's Notes: One of the spring ephemerals, Round-lobed Hepatica retains its leaves all winter and quickly sends up flowers each spring before the trees above have a chance to produce leaves and shade it out. Previous year's leaves are dark purple to brown, while new growth is a light green. Called "Hepatica" because the lobes of the leaves resemble the three lobes of the liver, which early herbalists interpreted to mean that this plant was good for treatment of liver troubles–not true. Nearly identical to Sharp-lobed Hepatica (pg.13), which has pointed lobed leaves. Also called Liverleaf. The stems of pollinated flowers lengthen and droop toward the ground where ants collect and disperse the seeds.

FLOWER TYPE   LEAF TYPE   LEAF ATTACHMENT

Regular   Simple Lobed

Basal

SHARP-LOBED HEPATICA
Hepatica acutiloba

Family: Buttercup (Ranunculaceae)

Height: 4-6" (10-15 cm)

Flower: flowers have 5-9 petal-like sepals that range in color from pale blue to white, lavender and pink, and have 3 green bracts underneath; each flower, ½-1" (1-2.5 cm) wide, sits on a single hairy stalk that may droop

Leaf: each basal leaf has 3 sharply pointed lobes rising from a thin hairy stalk

Bloom: spring

Cycle/Origin: perennial, native

Habitat: dry, shade, deciduous woods

Range: throughout, but more common in southern half

Stan's Notes: One of the spring ephemerals, Sharp-lobed Hepatica retains its leaves all winter and quickly sends up flowers each spring before the trees above have a chance to produce leaves and shade it out. Previous year's leaves are dark purple to brown, while new growth is a light green. Called "Hepatica" because the lobes of the leaves resemble the three lobes of the liver, which early herbalists interpreted to mean that this plant was good for treatment of liver troubles–not true. Also called Liverleaf. Nearly identical to Round-lobed Hepatica (pg. 11), which has rounded lobed leaves. The stems of pollinated flowers lengthen and droop toward the ground where ants collect and disperse the seeds.

FLOWER TYPE	LEAF TYPE	LEAF ATTACHMENT

Regular	Simple Lobed	Basal

HAREBELL
Campanula rotundifolia

Family: Bellflower (Campanulaceae)

Height: 6-20" (15-50 cm)

Flower: pale blue bell-shaped flowers, ¾" (2 cm) long, each formed from 5 fused petals and found nodding from a thin stem

Leaf: round basal leaves, ½-1" (1-2.5 cm) wide, that often wither before flowering, and linear grass-like leaves, 3" (7.5 cm) long and ⅛-¼" (.3-.6 cm) wide, alternate along the stem

Bloom: summer

Cycle/Origin: perennial, native

Habitat: wet, sun, rocky outcroppings along rivers, meadows, prairies

Range: throughout

Stan's Notes: Also called Bluebell, the Harebell, one of several species of *Campanula* found in Minnesota, is the smallest member with the thinnest and weakest stem. Its basal leaves are round, hence the species name, *rotundifolia* (round leaf). Like other members of this genus, its stems exude a milky sap. Its drooping flowers are adapted for specific insect pollination and also protect the pollen from rain and dew. The Harebell often grows in clumps and does well in gardens, but please don't dig it from the wild. This circumpolar plant grows at similar latitudes all around the world.

FLOWER TYPE	LEAF TYPE	LEAF ATTACHMENT	LEAF ATTACHMENT
Bell	Simple	Alternate	Basal

LARGE-LEAVED ASTER
Eurybia macrophylla

Family: Aster (Asteraceae)

Height: 1-5' (30-150 cm)

Flower: delicate, pale blue (sometimes white) flowers, 1" (2.5 cm) wide, each with 10-20 petals (ray flowers) and a yellow center (disk flowers) that turns red with age; 2-20 flowers per plant grow on a purplish stem

Leaf: large, coarsely toothed, heart-shaped basal leaves, soft to touch, 4-8" (10-20 cm) long, that are deeply notched where they attach to the stalk; smaller, stalkless, lance-shaped leaves alternate along the stem (cauline)

Bloom: summer, fall

Cycle/Origin: perennial, native

Habitat: dry, shade, deciduous woods

Range: north and east of the Twin Cities

Stan's Notes: A very common plant of the BWCA, the Large-leaved Aster sometimes carpets the ground, excluding other plants. Only about one in 50 plants sends up a flower stalk each year. The plant reproduces along a horizontal underground root system (rhizomes). Its flower stalks are sticky to the touch because of miniature glands. Because of their size and availability, the large leaves of this plant are often used as emergency toilet paper.

FLOWER TYPE	LEAF TYPE	LEAF ATTACHMENT	LEAF ATTACHMENT
Composite	Simple	Alternate	Basal

TALL BELLFLOWER
Campanulastrum americanum

Family: Bellflower (Campanulaceae)

Height: 3-6' (90-180 cm)

Flower: a single spike cluster, 1-2' (30-60 cm) long; individual flowers, 1" (2.5 cm) wide, are light blue with a white ring in the center of the flower (throat); each flower is made up of 5 pointed (and often twisted) petals

Leaf: pointed, toothed lance-shaped leaves, 3-6" (7.5-15 cm) long

Bloom: summer

Cycle/Origin: perennial, native

Habitat: wet, shade, deciduous woods, along forest edges

Range: southern half of the state

Stan's Notes: A tall flower of the shady borders of deciduous woods, Tall Bellflower is one of the tallest members of the Bellflower family. Its regular flowers are unusual because most other members in this family have tube or bell-like flowers.

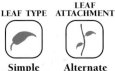

CLUSTER TYPE	FLOWER TYPE	LEAF TYPE	LEAF ATTACHMENT
Spike	Regular	Simple	Alternate

VIRGINIA BLUEBELLS
Mertensia virginica

Family: Borage (Boraginaceae)

Height: 10-24" (25-60 cm)

Flower: groups of light blue, elongated bell-shaped flowers; each flower, 1" (2.5 cm) long, has 5 petals that fuse into a long tube (corolla)

Leaf: basal leaves, 8" (20 cm) long, are much longer than stem leaves, 2-4" (5-10 cm) long; bluish green stem leaves (cauline) are alternately attached, smooth, round and toothless

Bloom: spring

Cycle/Origin: perennial, native

Habitat: wet, shade, in clearings and along the edges of deciduous woods

Range: southeastern corner of the state

Stan's Notes: Also called Lungwort, Virginia Cowslip or Hokoh Bluebells; Virginia Bluebells is a wonderful, pale blue, spring wildflower found in the southeastern portion of the state. Its flower buds begin pink but turn to light blue as flowers bloom, and its semi-succulent leaves have deep veins. A northern species (*M. paniculata*) grows along the North Shore of Lake Superior and has pointed leaves that are covered with fine hairs.

FLOWER TYPE	LEAF TYPE	LEAF ATTACHMENT	LEAF ATTACHMENT
Bell	Simple	Alternate	Basal

BIRD'S-FOOT VIOLET
Viola pedata

Family: Violet (Violaceae)

Height: 4-10" (10-25 cm)

Flower: deep-to-pale blue flowers, 1½" (4 cm) wide, each with 5 distinct petals; the lower petals are wider than the upper, but all have a white-lined throat with a small orange center; the flowers usually stand up above the leaves on their own stalk

Leaf: characteristically, narrowly lobed leaves, 1-2" (2.5-5 cm) wide, that resemble a bird's foot; each of the 3 main lobes are themselves lobed; each leaf rises from the base of the plant on its own stalk

Bloom: spring

Cycle/Origin: perennial, native

Habitat: dry, sunny fields, prairies, open woods

Range: southeastern quarter of state

Stan's Notes: One of almost 80 species of violet found in North America (and over 900 worldwide), the Bird's-foot Violet looks similar to the Prairie Violet. The Prairie Violet, however, has darker blue petals and a less pronounced orange center. Like all violets, they are highly variable and related to the annual pansy. Fortunately, its "bird's foot" leaves make it one of the easiest violets to identify. Look for it in cracks of rocks and in dry open fields. This plant is a host plant for the Fritillary butterfly.

FLOWER TYPE	LEAF TYPE	LEAF ATTACHMENT
Irregular	Simple Lobed	Basal

23

flower

CHICORY
Cichorium intybus

Family: Aster (Asteraceae)

Height: 1-4' (30-120 cm)

Flower: sky blue stalkless flowers, 1½" (4 cm) wide, each with up to 20 petals (ray flowers) sparsely populate a tall stem and close by early afternoon; petals (ray flower) are square-tipped and fringed; the color ranges from white to pink, depending upon age and location

Leaf: long, toothed basal leaves similar to those of a dandelion, 3-6" (7.5-15 cm) long; stem leaves (cauline) are oblong and much smaller, ½-1" (1-2.5 cm) long, lack teeth and clasp the stem

Bloom: summer, fall

Cycle/Origin: perennial, non-native

Habitat: dry, sun, along roads, open fields

Range: southern half of the state, but can also be found near cities in northern Minnesota

Stan's Notes: Also known as Blue Sailor or Ragged Sailor, the Chicory's few flowers open one at a time and last only one day. This European import, believed to come from Eurasia, was brought to the U.S. to be cultivated for its long taproot, which can be roasted and ground as a coffee substitute or additive. Its leaves, like those of the dandelion, are edible, high in vitamins and minerals, but quite bitter.

FLOWER TYPE	LEAF TYPE	LEAF ATTACHMENT	LEAF ATTACHMENT	LEAF ATTACHMENT
Composite	Simple	Alternate	Basal	Clasping

BOTTLE GENTIAN
Gentiana andrewsii

Family: Gentian (Gentianaceae)

Height: 1-2' (30-60 cm)

Flower: a round, dense cluster of blue closed-tube flowers, 1-1½" (2.5-4 cm) long, sits atop the plant; each flower is made up of 5 fused petals that provide no apparent entrance into the flower

Leaf: toothless, lance-shaped leaves with 3 main veins; their sides bend upwards to form a trough; opposite leaves lower and whorled leaves near each flower cluster

Fruit: papery pod, roughly the size and shape of the flowers, contains hundreds of tiny brown seeds

Bloom: summer, fall

Cycle/Origin: perennial, native

Habitat: moist, sun, prairies, along railroad beds, old fields

Range: throughout

Stan's Notes: The Bottle Gentian is also called the Closed Gentian due to its curiously closed flowers, which keep out all but the largest insects. Bumblebees force themselves inside the flower through the top by pushing apart the petals. A wonderful perennial of the prairie, also called Prairie Gentian, this wildflower can also be grown in a garden—but please do not dig it from the wild. One of at least seven species of gentian in Minnesota.

FLOWER TYPE	LEAF TYPE	LEAF ATTACHMENT	LEAF ATTACHMENT	FRUIT
Tube	Simple	Opposite	Whorl	Pod

Virginia Waterleaf
Hydrophyllum virginianum

Family: Waterleaf (Hydrophyllaceae)

Height: 1-2' (30-60 cm)

Flower: round cluster, 1-1½" (2.5-4 cm) wide, of light blue-to-white, bell-shaped flowers, each ¼-½" (.6-1 cm) long; each flower has 5 petals that fuse to form a bell, and its inner flower parts conspicuously stick out beyond the petals

Leaf: large leaves, 5-6" (12.5-15 cm) long, with 5-7 sharply toothed lobes per leaf; leaves are often covered in white or gray "water spots"

Bloom: spring

Cycle/Origin: perennial, native

Habitat: moist deciduous woods

Range: throughout, except for the northern edge

Stan's Notes: A common plant of moist deciduous forests, Virginia Waterleaf often grows in large mats by reproducing along underground roots (rhizomes). Its leaves are often covered with white "water spots," hence the common name, "Waterleaf." The leaf spots are more obvious early in the spring and fade by early summer; the entire plant dies back to the ground by midsummer. A shade-loving plant that works well as ground cover or as fill-in for a shady yard or garden. Use a hand lens to view the center of the flower. The frilly stamens form a beautiful lavender pink lace.

CLUSTER TYPE	FLOWER TYPE	LEAF TYPE	LEAF ATTACHMENT
Round	Bell	Simple Lobed	Alternate

CREEPING BELLFLOWER
Campanula rapunculoides

Family: Bellflower (Campanulaceae)

Height: 1-3' (30-90 cm)

Flower: soft blue, bell-shaped flowers, 1-2" (2.5-5 cm) long, line up along a tall stem and almost always point downward; each flower is comprised of 5 sharply pointed petals fused together to form the bell-shaped flower

Leaf: heart-shaped lower leaves, 2" (5 cm) long, lance-shaped stem leaves (cauline) with fine teeth, ½-1" (1-2.5 cm) long

Fruit: downward-drooping pod-like containers hold many tiny seeds

Bloom: summer, fall

Growth: perennial, non-native

Habitat: dry, sun, fields, old homesteads

Range: throughout

Stan's Notes: Although native to Eurasia, the Creeping Bellflower is also called the European Bellflower and was undoubtedly introduced to the U.S. through Europe. A common garden plant 30 to 50 years ago, it has escaped cultivation and can now be found growing in the wild near old homesteads and abandoned gardens. It flowers only on one side of the stem. It spreads by underground roots and is often difficult to eliminate, once established.

FLOWER TYPE	LEAF TYPE	LEAF ATTACHMENT	FRUIT
	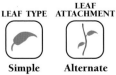		
Bell	Simple	Alternate	Pod

SPIDERWORT
Tradescantia occidentalis

Family: Spiderwort (Commelinaceae)

Height: 10-24" (25-60 cm)

Flower: a cluster of up to 10 flowers, each 1-2" (2.5-5 cm) wide, with 3 violet blue petals surrounding a golden yellow center; flowers open only a few at a time and are sometimes pink to white

Leaf: very long grass-like leaves, 15" (37.5 cm) long, clasp the stem; each leaf is folded lengthwise, forming a V-groove; long parallel veining

Bloom: spring, summer

Cycle/Origin: perennial, native

Habitat: dry, sun, meadows, fields, along roads, prairies

Range: throughout

Stan's Notes: An unusual-looking plant, Spiderwort's exotic flowers open in the morning and often wilt by noon on hot days. The wilted flowers sometimes leave a wet residue, giving it another common name, Widow's Tears. While "wort" means "common," "Spider" may refer to its mucilaginous sap, which strings out like a spider's web when the leaf is torn. It is also said that the plant's jointed stems appear like a giant spider's legs. When this plant is exposed to air pollution, its flowers change from blue to purple; therefore, it has recently been used as a natural barometer for air quality.

FLOWER TYPE	LEAF TYPE	LEAF ATTACHMENT	LEAF ATTACHMENT
Regular	Simple	Alternate	Clasping

PASQUEFLOWER
Pulsatilla patens

Family: Buttercup (Ranunculaceae)

Height: 4-10" (10-25 cm)

Flower: pale blue-to-white (rarely purple) flower, 1-2" (2.5-5 cm) wide, with 5-7 petal-like sepals surrounding a yellow center; grows on a single, densely haired stem

Leaf: long-stalked, deeply lobed, basal leaves, along with stalkless whorled leaves, present just beneath the flower; each leaf is deeply divided with very narrow lobes, ⅛" (.3 cm) wide, and covered in long silky hairs that make it look gray

Bloom: early spring

Cycle/Origin: perennial, native

Habitat: dry, sun, prairies

Range: southern half of state, northwest corner of state

Stan's Notes: Also called Crocus, the Pasqueflower is one of the earliest plants to bloom in Minnesota, usually only found in native prairies on sunny slopes. The entire plant, including the flowers, is covered with silvery soft hairs that may trap warm air next to the plant in the cool spring air. The common name is derived from its blooming time, often during the Easter (Paschal) season. Has long, feathery, plume-like hairs, 1-2" (2.5-5 cm), that carry seeds away on the wind.

FLOWER TYPE	LEAF TYPE	LEAF ATTACHMENT	LEAF ATTACHMENT
Regular	Simple Lobed	Basal	Whorl

HEAL-ALL
Prunella vulgaris

Family: Mint (Lamiaceae)

Height: 6-12" (15-30 cm)

Flower: thick compact spikes, 1-2" (2.5-5 cm) long, of violet-blue flowers; individual flowers, ½" (1 cm) long, have upper petals forming a hood, while lower petals form a landing platform (lip) for insects

Leaf: lance-shaped toothless leaves, 1-3" (2.5-7.5 cm) long, with short leafstalks; leaves sometimes have tiny wing-like leaves, ⅓" (.8 cm) long, growing from the point of attachment

Bloom: spring, summer, fall

Cycle/Origin: perennial, non-native

Habitat: wet, shade, lawns, fields, along roads

Range: throughout

Stan's Notes: Also called Self-heal and All-heal. The common names refer to this plant's use as a folk medicine in many cultures throughout the world. It is most commonly used in throat remedies, but little evidence of its effectiveness exists. Heal-all grows in large patches in lawns (where it prefers light shade) and will adapt to being mowed, forming a very low plant 2" (5 cm) tall. Like most members of the Mint family, Heal-all has a square stem and opposing leaves and emits a faint odor when crushed.

CLUSTER TYPE	FLOWER TYPE	LEAF TYPE	LEAF ATTACHMENT
Spike	Irregular	Simple	Opposite

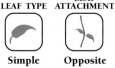

ALFALFA
Medicago sativa

Family: Pea or Bean (Fabaceae)

Height: 1-3' (30-90 cm)

Flower: tight spike clusters of blue flowers, 1-2" (2.5-5 cm) long; individual flowers, ¼-⅓" (.6-.8 cm) long, have 1 large upper petal and 3 smaller lower petals

Leaf: 3-part clover-like leaf, 1-2" (2.5-5 cm) long

Fruit: green seedpods twist into coils and become nearly black with age

Bloom: spring, summer, fall

Cycle/Origin: perennial, non-native

Habitat: dry, sun, fields, along roads

Range: throughout

Stan's Notes: This deep-rooted perennial is usually found along roads or fields where it has escaped cultivation. Alfalfa is often planted by farmers as a food crop for farm animals and to improve soil fertility (it fixes nitrogen from the air into the soil through its roots). A winter-hardy variety of alfalfa, developed by Wendeline Grimm in Carver County, Minnesota, in the late 1800s, was partially responsible for the establishment of the dairy industry in the upper Midwest in the early 1900s. Alfalfa's thin stems often cause the plant to fall over under its own weight at maturity, leaving it prostrate. Its flower color ranges from dark purple to light blue and it is a prime host plant for the alfalfa butterfly, Orange Sulphur.

CLUSTER TYPE	FLOWER TYPE	LEAF TYPE	LEAF ATTACHMENT	FRUIT
		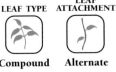		
Spike	Irregular	Compound	Alternate	Pod

GIANT BLUE HYSSOP
Agastache foeniculum

Family: Mint (Lamiaceae)

Height: 2-4' (60-120 cm)

Flower: a thick spike cluster, 1-3" (2.5-7.5 cm) long, of many light blue flowers; individual flowers, ¼" (.6 cm) long, are tightly packed together to give the appearance of 1 large single spike flower

Leaf: sharply pointed, lance-shaped, toothed leaves, 2-3" (5-7.5 cm) long, often whitish underneath, attached with a short leafstalk

Bloom: summer

Cycle/Origin: perennial, native

Habitat: dry, sun or shade, deciduous woods, prairies

Range: throughout

Stan's Notes: One of the largest members of the Mint family, the Giant Blue Hyssop, like all mints, has a square four-sided stem. Its opposing leaves smell strongly of anise (black licorice) when crushed, and make a very pleasant licorice-flavored tea. The Giant Blue Hyssop grows well in gardens but usually falls over by the end of summer. Spreads by producing hundreds of tiny black seeds. It blooms at the same time as Black-eyed Susans, resulting in a beautiful color combination. Flowers are very attractive to bees.

CLUSTER TYPE	FLOWER TYPE	LEAF TYPE	LEAF ATTACHMENT
Spike	Tube	Simple	Opposite

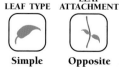

LEAD PLANT
Amorpha canescens

Family: Pea or Bean (Fabaceae)

Height: 1-3' (30-90 cm); shrub

Flower: a tight spike cluster, 1-3" (2.5-7.5 cm) long, of many small blue flowers; individual flowers, ⅛" (.4 cm) long, with protruding orange centers

Leaf: a single leaf, 1-3" (2.5-7.5 cm) long, is divided up into as many as 50 leaflets, ½" (1 cm) wide and ¾" (2 cm) long; leaves are covered with fine gray hairs, giving them a woolly grayish appearance

Bloom: spring, summer

Cycle/Origin: perennial, native

Habitat: dry, sun, prairies

Range: throughout, except for the Arrowhead Region

Stan's Notes: A woody shrub of dry prairies, Lead Plant can live for centuries and still not grow larger than 3' (90 cm) tall. Its large stringy root system gathers any available water and is sometimes called Prairie Shoestring. Roots dwell deep into the prairie soil, up to 10' (3 m) into the ground. Many parts of the plant have been used in folk medicine and a tea can be made from its leaves. The genus name, *Amorpha*, comes from the Greek *amorphos* (deformed), and refers to its single petal flower, which is not typical of the Pea or Bean family. Named "Lead Plant" because it grew on the dry soils overlaying lead ore deposits in southeastern Wisconsin.

CLUSTER TYPE	LEAF TYPE	LEAF ATTACHMENT
Spike	Compound	Alternate

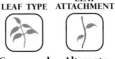

43

FRINGED GENTIAN
Gentianopsis crinita

Family: Gentian (Gentianaceae)

Height: 1-3' (30-90 cm)

Flower: deep violet blue flowers, 2" (5 cm) long, 1 per stalk, with blue-tipped green sepals surrounding 4 elongated petals that form the flower tube; each petal is frayed or fringed on the end

Leaf: lance-shaped toothless leaves, 1-2" (2.5-5 cm) long, with a round base nearly clasp the stem; prominent central vein ends at a pointed tip

Bloom: summer, fall

Cycle/Origin: biennial, native

Habitat: wet, prairies, meadows, along streams

Range: throughout

Stan's Notes: A spectacular flower of prairies, the Fringed Gentian is a true biennial that takes two years to bloom and should never be picked or dug up. One of the last wildflowers to bloom, it waits until late summer or autumn to produce flowers. Its ragged petal tips provide the first part of its common name. The second part, "Gentian," comes from King Gentius of Illyria, who discovered some medicinal properties in its roots. The Fringed Gentian is often found growing in wet spots within native prairies. The flower relies on a mycorrhizal relationship, the lack of which directly affects the presence or abundance of this wildflower.

FLOWER TYPE	LEAF TYPE	LEAF ATTACHMENT
Tube	Simple	Opposite

WILD BLUE PHLOX
Phlox divaricata

Family: Phlox (Polemoniaceae)

Height: 10-20" (25-50 cm)

Flower: flat clusters, 2-3" (5-7.5 cm) wide, of pale blue flowers; individual flowers, 1" (2.5 cm) wide, are made up of 5 petals fused together at the base into a short tube

Leaf: toothless, lance-shaped leaves, 1-2" (2.5-5 cm) long, grow opposite along the stem without a leafstalk

Bloom: spring, summer

Cycle/Origin: perennial, native

Habitat: wet, shade, deciduous woods

Range: southern half of the state

Stan's Notes: Also called Wood Phlox or Blue Phlox, Wild Blue Phlox is a single-stemmed woodland wildflower that grows in the dappled sunlight of the forest floor. Its fragrant flowers are occasionally white or dark blue, and its stems are often hairy and sticky to the touch. It is closely related to garden phlox. Closed flower buds have twisted petals appearing like a torch; the name "Phlox" is Greek for "flame." This plant blooms around Mother's Day and in bygone years, was often picked to add to wildflower bouquets for Mother.

CLUSTER TYPE	FLOWER TYPE	LEAF TYPE	LEAF ATTACHMENT
		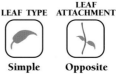	
Flat	Regular	Simple	Opposite

BLUE VERVAIN
Verbena hastata

Family: Vervain (Verbenaceae)

Height: 2-6' (60-180 cm)

Flower: tall thin spikes, 2-5" (5-12.5 cm) long, of small, deep blue, tube-like flowers, ⅛" (.3 cm) long; 5 petals fuse at the base to form a short tube

Leaf: matched pairs of narrow, lance-shaped, toothed leaves, 4-6" (10-15 cm) long; lower leaves are sometimes 3-lobed

Bloom: summer

Cycle/Origin: perennial, native

Habitat: wet, along ditches, shores, wet fields, roadsides

Range: throughout

Stan's Notes: Blue Vervain is a tall slender plant with multiple pencil-thin flower spikes that bloom from the bottom up. Its stems are square with opposite leaves, which is why it is often confused with a member of the Mint family. The genus name, *Verbena*, is Latin for "sacred plant," and refers to an ancient time when the plant was thought to have medicinal properties. It rarely produces a pink flower and is often confused with Hoary Vervain (pg. 145). Visited by many butterflies and bees for its high nectar content.

CLUSTER TYPE	FLOWER TYPE	LEAF TYPE	LEAF ATTACHMENT
Spike	**Regular**	**Simple**	**Opposite**

BLUE FLAG IRIS
Iris versicolor

Family: Iris (Iridaceae)

Height: 2-3' (60-90 cm)

Flower: several large blue or violet flowers, 2½-4" (6-10 cm) wide, rising on tall stiff stalks; the center of the lowest petals (sepals) are beardless (no bristles) with a white patch (throat) trimmed in yellow

Leaf: narrow grass-like blades, 1" (2.5 cm) wide and 8-32" (20-80 cm) long; similar to garden irises

Fruit: large green pod, 1½-2" (4-5 cm) long, with round ends containing multiple seeds

Bloom: spring, summer

Cycle/Origin: perennial, native

Habitat: wet, sun or shade, edges of wetlands, lakes and rivers

Range: throughout

Stan's Notes: Also called the Northern Iris, this wildflower is usually found along water growing in clumps of tall, erect, sword-like leaves with many flowers. These clumps are created by a toxic, horizontal, underground root (rhizome) which many cultures have used as medicine. Its largest petals are actually modified leaves (sepals). Insects entering the flower must walk along the sepals and pass under the plant's male and female flower parts, thus completing pollination. "Iris" is derived from the Greek word for "rainbow," and describes the wide range of flower colors in the Iris family.

FLOWER TYPE	LEAF TYPE	LEAF ATTACHMENT	FRUIT
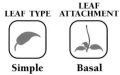			
Irregular	Simple	Basal	Pod

WILD LUPINE
Lupinus perennis

Family: Pea or Bean (Fabaceae)

Height: 1-3' (30-90 cm)

Flower: a spike, 3-7" (7.5-18 cm) long, of blue pea-like flowers, each ⅔" (1.6 cm) wide; what appear to be 3 petals (called, from the top down, standard, wing and keel) are actually 5 petals fused together

Leaf: leaf stems arise from base of the plant and end with a palmate leaf, 5-10" (12.5-25 cm) wide, made of 7-11 small leaflets

Fruit: initially many green, fuzzy, pea-pod-shaped fruits, up to 2" (5 cm) long, turn black when mature, contain 10-20 small brown-to-black seeds

Bloom: late spring, early summer

Cycle/Origin: perennial, native

Habitat: dry, sandy soils in open woods, mostly in sunny fields or along roads, prairies

Range: southeastern half of the state

Stan's Notes: These pea-like flowers open under the weight of an insect, revealing a horned-shaped stamen that deposits pollen on its visitor. This is the only host plant for the Karner Blue butterfly caterpillar, an endangered species in Minnesota. A closely related garden escapee (*L. polyphyllus*) has multicolored flowers and grows in dense clusters (see inset photo).

CLUSTER TYPE	FLOWER TYPE	LEAF TYPE	LEAF ATTACHMENT	FRUIT

Spike	Irregular	Palmate	Basal	Pod

PICKERELWEED
Pontederia cordata

Family: Pickerelweed (Pontederiaceae)

Height: aquatic

Flower: many spike clusters, 4-6" (10-15 cm) long, of blue flowers; individual flowers, ½" (1 cm) long, have 3 upper petals (the middle upper petal has 2 small yellow spots) and 3 lower petals

Leaf: pointed, toothless, heart-shaped leaves, 4-10" (10-25 cm) long, rise from an underwater root; each leaf is indented at the base, where the stalk attaches

Bloom: summer

Cycle/Origin: perennial, native

Habitat: lakes, wetlands, ponds, streams

Range: eastern half of the state

Stan's Notes: An aquatic plant that forms large mats, Pickerelweed's leaves and flowers rise above the water (it is rooted to the bottom of lakes). The common name refers to the Pickerel, a fish that shares a similar watery habitat. Leaves are similar to Arrowhead (pg. 197), but flowers are completely different in color, size and shape. Prefers shallow water, unlike the deep-water-loving White Water Lily (pg. 301) and the Yellow Water Lily (pg. 385). Visited by a small solitary bee, *Halictoides noval-angliae*, which visits this plant only for nectar and pollen.

CLUSTER TYPE	FLOWER TYPE	LEAF TYPE	LEAF ATTACHMENT
	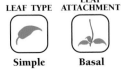		
Spike	Irregular	Simple	Basal

FALSE INDIGO
Baptisia australis

Family: Pea or Bean (Fabaceae)

Height: 3-5' (90-150 cm)

Flower: irregular, dark blue, pea-like flowers, ½-1" (1-2.5 cm) long, alternate along the stem to form spike clusters up to 10" (25 cm) long; flowers sit perpendicular to the stem; only large insects are heavy enough to open them and get inside to sip nectar

Leaf: gray green leaves, 1-3" (2.5-7.5 cm) long, composed of 3 leaflets; each leaflet is pointed near the base and wider at the tip

Fruit: a green pod, 1-3" (2.5-7.5 cm) long, that turns black and papery with age and splits open lengthwise to release small, round, brown seeds

Bloom: summer

Cycle/Origin: perennial, non-native

Habitat: dry, sun, open fields, prairies, along roads

Range: southern half of the state

Stan's Notes: The False Indigo is a shrub-like perennial that dies into the ground each year. Once a favorite garden flower, it has escaped to the wild. The genus name, *Baptisia*, comes from the Greek *baptizein* (to dye), and refers to its sap, which turns purple when exposed to the air. The poor quality of the indigo dye obtained from this plant provides the "False" part of its name.

CLUSTER TYPE	FLOWER TYPE	LEAF TYPE	LEAF ATTACHMENT	FRUIT

Spike	Irregular	Compound	Alternate	Pod

WILD GINGER
Asarum canadense

Family: Birthwort (Aristolochiaceae)

Height: 6-12" (15-30 cm)

Flower: a single, brown-to-greenish red, tube-shaped flower, 1-2" (2.5-5 cm) long, with 3 pointed lobes; located between 2 leafstalks at ground level

Leaf: a pair of large heart-shaped leaves, 3-6" (7.5-15 cm) wide; each leaf is soft and velvety due to dense hairs and has a deep notch where the stalk attaches

Bloom: spring

Cycle/Origin: perennial, native

Habitat: moist, shade, deciduous woods

Range: throughout

Stan's Notes: Wild Ginger's large flowers are located at ground level to accommodate ground-dwelling insects, such as beetles, that pollinate its flower. Its stems and leaves are covered with long white hairs, and each plant has a single flower located between the pair of leafstalks. It grows from a long horizontal rootstock and has a strong ginger-like odor when crushed (it is not, however, the same species of ginger that is used in Asian cooking).

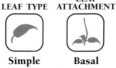

FLOWER TYPE — Tube

LEAF TYPE — Simple

LEAF ATTACHMENT — Basal

GROUNDNUT
Apios americana

Family: Pea or Bean (Fabaceae)

Height: 3-10' (90-300 cm); climbing vine

Flower: a round (sometimes spiked) cluster, 2-4" (5-10 cm) long, of small, brown-purple, waxy flowers, ½" (1 cm) wide; each cluster rises from a leaf attachment (axis) and is made up of 5-10 very fragrant flowers; each flower has 5 fused petals

Leaf: leaves, 6" (15 cm) long, usually made up of 5-7 pointed leaflets

Bloom: summer

Cycle/Origin: perennial, native

Habitat: wet, sun or shade, shrubby borders

Range: southern two-thirds of the state

Stan's Notes: A legume of the forest edge, the Groundnut is a climbing vine that covers other vegetation as it grows. Late in summer, the plant displays large clusters of very fragrant brown-purple flowers. The plant's long stringy roots produce small edible tubers similar to tiny potatoes, hence its common name. Native Americans once gathered its tubers for food, and many historians believe that Groundnuts were eaten by Pilgrims during their first winters in the New World. Its genus name, *Apios*, comes from the Greek word for "pear," referring to the shape of its underground tubers.

CLUSTER TYPE	FLOWER TYPE	LEAF TYPE	LEAF ATTACHMENT
Round	Irregular	Compound	Alternate

ABORTED BUTTERCUP
Ranunculus abortivus

Family: Buttercup (Ranunculaceae)

Height: 6-24" (15-60 cm)

Flower: a tall thin-stemmed plant with inconspicuous, cone-shaped green flowers, ¼" (.6 cm) long, with 5 extremely tiny, nearly "aborted" yellow petals

Leaf: round or kidney-shaped basal leaves, 1-1½" (2.5-4 cm) wide, with scalloped teeth; stem leaves (cauline) have 3-5 deep lobes and attach alternately on the stem; 1 leaf at each branching

Bloom: spring, summer

Cycle/Origin: annual, native

Habitat: moist woodlands, usually in the shade of large, mature deciduous trees

Range: throughout

Stan's Notes: Also called the Kidney-leaf Buttercup because of its kidney-shaped basal leaves. This atypical buttercup received the name "Aborted" because of its extremely tiny yellow flower petals (it is also known as the Small-flowered Buttercup for the same reason). The Aborted Buttercup's round basal leaves and tiny yellow petals help identify it. The flower lacks any nectar; instead, it rewards visiting insects with nutritious pollen.

FLOWER TYPE	LEAF TYPE	LEAF TYPE	LEAF ATTACHMENT	LEAF ATTACHMENT
Regular	Simple	Simple Lobed	Alternate	Basal

PINEAPPLE-WEED
Matricaria discoidea

Family: Aster (Asteraceae)

Height: 3-8" (7.5-20 cm)

Flower: several (often many) small, green-to-yellow dome-shaped flowers, ¼" (.6 cm) tall

Leaf: individual leaves highly divided into thin, parsley-like leaves, ½-1" (1-2.5 cm) long

Bloom: summer, fall

Cycle/Origin: annual, native

Habitat: dry, sun, along roads, disturbed soils, farmyards

Range: throughout

Stan's Notes: A small inconspicuous plant that grows in disturbed soils along sidewalks, roads and gardens, the Pineapple-weed is so named because its flowers and leaves smell strongly of pineapple when crushed. It also makes a delicious yellow tea. A type of aster, it has a composite flower only of disk flowers, lacking petals (ray flowers). A close relative to the Wild Chamomile, which has white daisy-like petals (ray flowers).

FLOWER TYPE

Composite

LEAF TYPE

Simple Lobed

LEAF ATTACHMENT

Alternate

fruit

SMOOTH SOLOMON'S SEAL
Polygonatum biflorum

Family: Lily (Liliaceae)

Height: 1-3' (30-90 cm)

Flower: groups of 2-10, green, 6-petaled, bell-shaped flowers, ½-1" (1-2.5 cm) long, hang from short stalks, 1" (2.5 cm) long; flower stalks arise from a leaf base (axis)

Leaf: toothless, lance-shaped, stalkless leaves, 2-6" (5-15 cm) long, clasp an arching stem; conspicuous parallel veining makes the leaf look light green

Fruit: blue-to-black berries, ¼" (.6 cm) round

Bloom: spring

Cycle/Origin: perennial, native

Habitat: dry, shade, deciduous woods

Range: throughout

Stan's Notes: Also called True Solomon's Seal, this plant is distinguished by its long arching stems that grow up to 3' (90 cm) long. To remember the difference between True and False Solomon's Seal (pg. 299), use this rhyme: "Solomon's seal, to be real, must have flowers along its keel." Although the species name suggests two flowers (*bi*=two, *florum*=flower), it can grow up to ten flowers per leaf axis. The plant grows from a large underground rootstock (rhizome). When its stalk breaks away, it leaves a distinctive round mark resembling the seal of King Solomon. Native Americans gathered its roots for food, but the roots may leave one's mouth tingling and numb.

FLOWER TYPE	LEAF TYPE	LEAF ATTACHMENT	FRUIT
	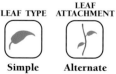		
Bell	**Simple**	**Alternate**	**Berry**

BASTARD TOADFLAX
Comandra umbellata

Family: Sandalwood (Santalaceae)

Height: 6-16" (15-40 cm)

Flower: several compact, flat clusters, 1-2" (2.5-5 cm) wide, of greenish white flowers; individual flowers, 1/6" (.5 cm) long; 5 petal-like sepals fuse at base

Leaf: small oval leaves, 3/4-1½" (2-4 cm) wide, alternately line the stem; pale green underneath

Bloom: spring, summer

Growth: perennial, native

Habitat: dry, open fields

Range: throughout

Stan's Notes: The Bastard Toadflax is a semiparasitic plant, obtaining some of its nutrients from the roots of other plants, although it also uses the sun to perform photosynthesis to make its own food. Its greenish white flowers lack any regular petals, displaying instead modified leaves called sepals. The name "Toad" has in the past been used to describe any plant that grows in the shade, but it also might come from "tod," a clump or tuft that would certainly describe this plant's flowering habit. This wildflower forms colonies along horizontal underground roots (rhizomes).

CLUSTER TYPE

Flat

FLOWER TYPE

Regular

LEAF TYPE

Simple

LEAF ATTACHMENT

Alternate

WILD SARSAPARILLA
Aralia nudicaulis

Family: Ginseng (Araliaceae)

Height: 1-2' (30-60 cm)

Flower: 3 distinct round clusters, 1-2" (2.5-5 cm) wide, made of greenish white flowers; individual flowers, ¼" (.6 cm) long, have 5 tiny white petals

Leaf: 2 main stalks, each of which spreads into 3 leafstalks that grow 3-5 fine-toothed oval leaflets, 3-4" (7.5-10 cm) long, with pointed ends

Fruit: clusters of round purple-to-black berries, ⅛" (.3 cm), on a leafless stalk

Bloom: summer

Cycle/Origin: perennial, native

Habitat: dry, shade, conifer woods, deciduous woods

Range: throughout

Stan's Notes: A perennial of conifer and deciduous woodlands, just about every part of Wild Sarsaparilla comes in threes, including leaf stems, leaflets and flower stalks. Its horizontal underground roots are very aromatic and have been used as a substitute for sarsaparilla in root beer. Its clusters of purple-to-black berries are eaten by wildlife, and its leaves usually rise well above the flowers, often concealing them. The species name, *nudicaulis*, comes from the Latin *nudus* (naked) and *cauli* (stalk), and refers to the plant's leafless flower stalk.

CLUSTER TYPE	FLOWER TYPE	LEAF TYPE	LEAF ATTACHMENT	FRUIT
Round	Regular	Compound	Basal	Berry

fruit

BLUE COHOSH
Caulophyllum thalictroides

Family: Barberry (Berberidaceae)

Size: 1-3' (30-90 cm)

Flower: a round cluster, 2" (5 cm) wide, of up to 20 greenish yellow flowers; individual flowers, ½" (1 cm) wide, have 6 pointed, petal-like sepals surrounding 6 smaller rounded petals

Leaf: a leaf is divided into several stalks and as many as 27 small leaflets; each leaflet, 1-3" (2.5-7.5 cm) long, has 3-5 pointed lobes; in spring, leaves and stems are often purplish blue in color

Fruit: dark blue berry on a thick stalk

Bloom: spring

Cycle/Origin: perennial, native

Habitat: wet, deciduous woods, shade

Range: throughout

Stan's Notes: A shade-loving plant of the deciduous forest, Blue Cohosh flowers range in color from greenish yellow to purplish brown. An erect, single main stem, purplish blue in color in spring, is covered with a light dusting of white powder that is easily wiped off. The poisonous blue berries sit atop a characteristically thickened stem and together they resemble a miniature light bulb. The leaves resemble those of Early Meadow Rue (pg. 283) or Tall Meadow Rue (pg. 295); hence the species name, *thalictroides*.

CLUSTER TYPE	FLOWER TYPE	LEAF TYPE	LEAF ATTACHMENT	FRUIT
Round	Regular	Compound	Alternate	Berry

73

fruit

JACK-IN-THE-PULPIT
Arisaema triphyllum

Family: Arum (Araceae)

Height: 1-3' (30-90 cm)

Flower: an erect club (spadix or "Jack"), 2-3" (5-7.5 cm) long, sits inside a green or purplish hood (spathe or "pulpit") at the top of a single stalk; base of the green club is lined with tiny separate male or female flowers, protected by the hood

Leaf: 1 or 2 (female plant has 2; male has 1) large, dull green, deep-veined, compound leaves, 5-12" (12.5-30 cm) long, made up of 3 leaflets

Fruit: cluster of shiny green berries that turn red in autumn

Bloom: spring

Cycle/Origin: perennial, native

Habitat: wet, shade, moist deciduous woods

Range: throughout

Stan's Notes: Also called Indian Turnip because Native Americans gathered its large taproots (corm) as food, this is not considered an edible plant. The plant, root and berries all contain calcium oxalate crystals, which cause a burning sensation in the mouth. Its large three-part leaves are often confused with Large-flowered Trillium leaves (pg. 289), but Jack-in-the-pulpit has a deep vein that runs around the leaf's entire margin. If disturbed or affected by other stress, the female plant declines in vigor and may stop producing fruit.

CLUSTER TYPE	LEAF TYPE	LEAF ATTACHMENT	FRUIT
	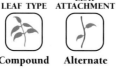		
Spike	**Compound**	**Alternate**	**Berry**

ALUMROOT
Heuchera richardsonii

Family: Saxifrage (Saxifragaceae)

Height: 2-3' (60-90 cm)

Flower: a spike cluster, 2-4" (5-10 cm) tall, of green-to-brown bell flowers, ¼" (.6 cm) wide, on a tall, thin leafless flower stalk; 5 petals form each bell-shaped flower

Leaf: maple-leaf-shaped basal leaves, 3-4" (7.5-10 cm) wide; hairy stalks; each leaf is coarsely toothed, hairy beneath, and made up of 3-5 lobes

Bloom: spring, summer

Cycle/Origin: perennial, native

Habitat: dry, prairies, along roads, fields, open woods, rock outcroppings

Range: throughout

Stan's Notes: Alumroot grows in a wide variety of habitats, from prairies to woodlands to rock outcroppings. Its thick root was used as an astringent in folk medicine, hence the common name, "Alum." The genus name, *Heuchera*, is in honor of Johan von Heucher, an eighteenth-century German physician and botanist. A similar species (*H. americana*) grows in shaded woodlands. A member of the Saxifrage family, the name comes from two Latin words that mean "rock" and "break," referring to its habit of growing in rock outcroppings.

CLUSTER TYPE	FLOWER TYPE	LEAF TYPE	LEAF ATTACHMENT
Spike	**Bell**	**Simple**	**Basal**

ORANGE HAWKWEED
Hieracium aurantiacum

Family: Aster (Asteraceae)

Height: 1-2' (30-60 cm)

Flower: 2-10 bright orange flower heads, ¾-1" (2-2.5 cm) wide, made up of 20-30 individual ray flowers, grow on a single stem; only a few open at a time

Leaf: simple, linear, toothless and stalkless, hair-covered leaves, 2-5" (5-12.5 cm) long, with rounded ends

Bloom: summer

Cycle/Origin: perennial, non-native

Habitat: dry, sun, fields, disturbed soils, pastures, along roads

Range: eastern edge of the state, especially along the North Shore of Lake Superior

Stan's Notes: Also called King-devil or Devil's Paintbrush, as its single stem is topped with a red orange color, resembling a painter's brush. This plant originated in Eurasia as an alpine plant. Now naturalized in North America, it is sometimes considered a noxious weed. It grows in large patches, spreading by above-ground runners. This single-stemmed plant will hold up to ten flower heads that close at night and on cloudy days. After pollination, its flowering heads produce a dandelion-like silk to carry away its seeds. The name "Hawkweed" came from the mistaken belief that hawks ate the flowers to improve their vision. Seven species of "Hawkweed" grow in Minnesota, and it is often mistaken for an orange daisy.

FLOWER TYPE

Composite

LEAF TYPE

Simple

LEAF ATTACHMENT

Basal

SPOTTED TOUCH-ME-NOT
Impatiens capensis

Family: Touch-me-not (Balsaminaceae)

Height: 3-5' (90-150 cm)

Flower: orange flowers, 1" (2.5 cm) long, covered with reddish brown spots; each flower has a large open mouth that leads to a long, thin, sharp-curved tube (spur)

Leaf: sharp-toothed, oval leaves, 1-3" (2.5-7.5 cm) long, alternate on short leafstalks, 1" (2.5 cm)

Fruit: thin, banana-shaped pod-like containers

Bloom: summer

Cycle/Origin: annual, native

Habitat: wet, shade, wetlands, along streams

Range: throughout

Stan's Notes: Also called Jewelweed because water droplets on its leaves shine like tiny jewels, the Spotted Touch-me-not is a tall annual plant of wet areas. Its stems are nearly translucent and contain a slippery juice that can be used to soothe the sting from nettles or Poison Ivy. Its long, thin, ripe seedpods explode when touched, throwing seeds in all directions. This action, combined with the dark spots on its flowers, provide the Spotted Touch-me-not's common name. A similar species, Pale Touch-me-not (*I. pallida*) also called Jewelweed (pg. 333), has yellow flowers that are not as spotted. Scrape off the ripe seed's dark brown covering to discover a sky blue seed inside. An important nectar plant for hummingbirds.

FLOWER TYPE	LEAF TYPE	LEAF ATTACHMENT	FRUIT
Tube	Simple	Alternate	Pod

HOARY PUCCOON
Lithospermum canescens

Family: Borage (Boraginaceae)

Height: 6-12" (15-30 cm)

Flower: flat cluster, 2-3" (5-7.5 cm) wide, of orange-to-yellow flowers; individual flowers, ½" (1 cm) wide, have 5 petals that form a small tube at the base; flower stem is in shape of a question mark

Leaf: nearly stalkless, narrow, hairy leaves, ½-1" (1-2.5 cm) long, alternate along a hairy stem

Bloom: spring

Cycle/Origin: perennial, native

Habitat: dry, sun, rocky soils, prairies, along roads

Range: throughout

Stan's Notes: Eighteen species of Puccoon are found in North America, but only four are in Minnesota, including Hoary Puccoon. This plant usually grows with only one main stem topped with a cluster of flowers. The fine grayish hairs that cover its stems and leaves give it the "Hoary" name. "Puccoon" is a Native American name for any plant used for color dye (the roots of the Puccoon make a red dye). This plant looks similar to the orange Butterfly-weed (pg. 85), although it's not generally as tall or robust.

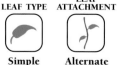

CLUSTER TYPE	FLOWER TYPE	LEAF TYPE	LEAF ATTACHMENT
Flat	Regular	Simple	Alternate

fruit

BUTTERFLY-WEED
Asclepias tuberosa

Family: Milkweed (Asclepiadaceae)

Height: 1-2' (30-60 cm)

Flower: a large, flat-topped cluster, 2-3" (5-7.5 cm) wide, made of small, individual orange flowers, ⅜" (.9 cm) wide, each with downward-curved petals

Leaf: hairy toothless leaves, 2-6" (5-15 cm) long, widen at tip

Fruit: erect small clusters of narrow pods, 6" (15 cm) long, covered in fine hairs; pods contain large brown seeds with silken "parachutes" to carry away each seed

Bloom: spring, summer

Cycle/Origin: perennial, native

Habitat: dry, sun, prairies, prefers sandy soils

Range: throughout, but mostly in the south and east

Stan's Notes: Found in prairies and along railroad beds growing in clumps, this true milkweed lacks milky sap; instead, its stem and leaves bleed clear sap. The species name, *tuberosa*, refers to its large taproot, which makes it nearly impossible to transplant (it can be grown from seed). Its single stems branch only near the top and its flower stalks harbor up to 25 individual flowers. Its flowers vary from all yellow to red, and its roots and stems have been used in folk medicine. A host plant for Gray Hairstreak and Monarch butterfly caterpillars.

CLUSTER TYPE	FLOWER TYPE	LEAF TYPE	LEAF ATTACHMENT	FRUIT
		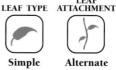		
Flat	**Irregular**	**Simple**	**Alternate**	**Pod**

PRAIRIE LILY
Lilium philadelphicum

Family: Lily (Liliaceae)

Height: 2-3' (60-90 cm)

Flower: large, upright, orange flowers, 2-3" (5-7.5 cm) wide, with 6 petals (actually 3 petals and 3 sepals), all covered with dark purplish spots on a faint yellow background; 1 to 8 flowers per plant

Leaf: a whorl of 4-7 narrow, lance-shaped leaves, 2-3" (5-7.5 cm) long

Fruit: oblong pod, 2" (5 cm) long

Bloom: summer

Cycle/Origin: perennial, native

Habitat: wet, sun, prairies, dry deciduous and conifer woods

Range: throughout

Stan's Notes: A showy lily of the prairie and woodland habitats, the Prairie Lily is the only upright-pointing lily that grows on the prairie. It is also called Wood Lily because it grows in dry deciduous and conifer woods. It grows from a large, scaly underground bulb.

FLOWER TYPE	LEAF TYPE	LEAF ATTACHMENT	FRUIT
Regular	Simple	Whorl	Pod

TURK'S-CAP LILY
Lilium superbum

Family: Lily (Liliaceae)

Height: 3-7' (90-210 cm)

Flower: large, dangling, orange-to-yellow flowers, 2-3" (5-7.5 cm) wide, with 6 backward-curving petals (actually 3 petals and 3 sepals), all covered with dark purplish spots and yellow centers that fade to orange); 1 to 8 flowers per plant

Leaf: a whorl of 4-6 narrow, lance-shaped leaves, 2-6" (5-15 cm) long

Fruit: oblong pod, 2" (5 cm) long

Bloom: summer

Cycle/Origin: perennial, native

Habitat: wet, sun, along roads in wet ditches, moist woods

Range: throughout

Stan's Notes: Also called Michigan Lily and once common along country roads, the Turk's-cap Lily has decreased due to the mowing and draining of ditches. A big showy lily that grows from a large, scaly underground bulb, it can grow up to 20 flowers per plant. The curled flower petals resemble a Turkish hat; hence the Turk's-cap Lily's common name. Native Americans once gathered its bulbs for food.

FLOWER TYPE
Regular

LEAF TYPE
Simple

LEAF ATTACHMENT
Whorl

FRUIT
Pod

FOUR-O'CLOCK
Mirabilis nyctaginea

Family: Four-o'clock (Nyctaginaceae)

Height: 1-3' (30-90 cm)

Flower: pink or purple flowers, ¼-½" (.6-1 cm) wide, made up of 5 notched petals fused together at the base; small clusters of flowers are set against a green shield called a bract

Leaf: pairs of heart-shaped leaves, 2-4" (5-10 cm) long, opposite on the stem

Bloom: spring, summer, fall

Cycle/Origin: annual or perennial, depending on location, native

Habitat: wet or dry, sun or shade, woodlands or disturbed soils, highly adaptive plant

Range: throughout

Stan's Notes: A single-stemmed plant that branches only near the top into flower stalks, the Four-o'clock's flowers open late in the afternoon (hence its common name) and last until the following day, usually wilting by noon. Blooming overnight suggests that it might be pollinated by night-flying insects, such as moths. Its stems are four-sided and smooth, and it often grows along roads or in disturbed soils and gardens. Three species of Four-o'clock can be found in Minnesota. In southern Minnesota, this plant is a perennial. In northern Minnesota where the climate is harsher, it grows only as an annual. It is visited by Sphinx Moths (also known as Hummingbird Moths) for its nectar.

FLOWER TYPE

Regular

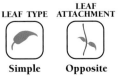

LEAF TYPE

Simple

LEAF ATTACHMENT

Opposite

fruit

ROSE TWISTED-STALK
Streptopus roseus

Family: Lily (Liliaceae)

Size: 1-3' (30-90 cm)

Flower: pink, bell-shaped flowers, ⅓" (.8 cm) long, with 6 petals hang on crooked, thread-like stalks from the main stem of the plant at each leaf joint (axil)

Leaf: lance-shaped leaves 2-3" (2.5-5 cm) long, with obvious parallel veins clasp the stem; edge of leaf (margin) fringed with minute hairs

Fruit: round red berry

Bloom: spring, summer

Cycle/Origin: perennial, native

Habitat: moist deciduous woods

Range: northern two-thirds of the state, from the Twin Cities north

Stan's Notes: A single arching stemmed plant of moist woodlands. The pink bell flowers produce bright red berries. Look for the characteristic twisted or zigzag stem. A single leaf attaches at each turn of the stem. The stem and the edges of the leaves are covered with minute hairs. The genus name breaks down to *Streptos* and *pous,* which are Greek for "twisted" and "foot" or "stalk;" hence its common name. The berries are mildly cathartic (cause diarrhea), so don't eat them.

FLOWER TYPE	LEAF TYPE	LEAF ATTACHMENT	LEAF ATTACHMENT	FRUIT
Bell	**Simple**	**Alternate**	**Clasping**	**Berry**

SPREADING DOGBANE
Apocynum androsaemifolium

Family: Dogbane (Apocynaceae)

Height: 1-4' (30-120 cm)

Flower: groups of 2-10 tiny, pink-to-white, bell-shaped flowers, ⅓" (.8 cm) long; individual flowers are white with pink stripes; 5 petals fuse together to form the bell

Leaf: simple, oval, toothless leaves, 2-4" (5-10 cm) long, often with a wavy edge

Fruit: long thin pods, 3-8" (7.5-20 cm), that open along 1 side, revealing seeds attached to long tufts of white fuzz

Bloom: summer

Cycle/Origin: perennial, native

Habitat: dry, sun, along roads, edges of deciduous woods

Range: throughout

Stan's Notes: A tall perennial plant with a single main stem that branches out into many "spreading" stems. A close relative of the milkweed, it produces a thick, white, milky juice in its stem and leaves; this juice contains cardiac glycosides that cause hot flashes, rapid heartbeat and fatigue. Insects avoid this plant because of the poisonous juice. When dried and peeled, the stem makes a strong cord, which was once used by Native Americans for fishing and trapping. The same fibers are selectively used by orioles as nest-building material.

FLOWER TYPE	LEAF TYPE	LEAF ATTACHMENT	FRUIT
	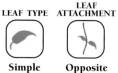		
Bell	Simple	Opposite	Pod

TWINFLOWER
Linnaea borealis

Family: Honeysuckle (Caprifoliaceae)

Height: 3-6" (7.5-15 cm)

Flower: a pair of small, pink, bell flowers, ½" (1 cm) long, each with 5 petals fused to form a bell; flowers hang from a single, thinly-forked stem

Leaf: small, round, toothless, evergreen leaves, ½" (1 cm) wide, paired low on the stem; leaves are light green and shiny

Bloom: summer

Cycle/Origin: perennial, native

Habitat: conifer woods, bogs, rock outcroppings

Range: northern half of the state, especially in the Arrowhead Region and BWCA

Stan's Notes: A low-growing evergreen plant, Twinflower forms patches by trailing stems along the ground and sending up short, thin flower stalks with a pair of leaves near the base and a pair or "twin set" of fragrant pink flowers. This common flower is found in northern conifer forests throughout the world (circumpolar). Its genus name, *Linnaea*, is in honor of the father of botany, C. Linnaeus (1707-1778), who developed the modern way of naming plants and animals by using two names of usually Latin, but sometimes Greek, derivation genus and species.

FLOWER TYPE

Bell

LEAF TYPE

Simple

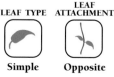

LEAF ATTACHMENT

Opposite

DAISY FLEABANE
Erigeron annuus

Family: Aster (Asteraceae)

Height: 1-5' (30-150 cm)

Flower: small pink (sometimes white) flower heads, ½" (1 cm) wide; up to 40 tiny petals (ray flowers) with a yellow center (disk flowers); individual plants can hold up to 30 flower heads

Leaf: thin, finely toothed, lance-shaped, hairy leaves, up to 5" (12.5 cm) long, alternate along a noticeably hairy stem; most leaves lack a stalk and larger leaves are clasping

Bloom: spring, summer, fall

Cycle/Origin: annual, native

Habitat: wet or dry, sun or shade, conifer woods, deciduous woods, old fields

Range: eastern half of the state

Stan's Notes: One of the first asters to bloom each spring, continuing to flower until autumn. An erect plant with thin hairy stems, often growing along roads and edges of woods. Its common name comes from its daisy-like flowers which, when dried, were once believed to keep away fleas. The genus name, *Erigeron*, comes from the Greek *eri* (early) and *geron* (old man), referring to the plant's early blooming and silvery appearance of its hairy stems. At least seven species of fleabane are found in Minnesota. Differentiated from other white-flowered asters by lack of leaves on flower stalks.

FLOWER TYPE	LEAF TYPE	LEAF ATTACHMENT	LEAF ATTACHMENT
Composite	Simple	Alternate	Clasping

99

CROWN VETCH
Securigera varia

Family: Pea or Bean (Fabaceae)

Height: 1-2' (30-60 cm); climbing vine

Flower: round clusters, 1" (2.5 cm) wide, of pink and white flowers; individual flowers ¼-½" (.6-1 cm) wide, are pea-like with pink upper petals (standard) and white side petals (wings)

Leaf: each leaf, 2-4" (5-10 cm) long, is made up of 12-25 round leaflets, ½-¾" (1-2 cm) wide

Fruit: flat pea-like pod, 1-2" (2.5-5 cm) long

Bloom: summer

Cycle/Origin: perennial, non-native

Habitat: dry, sun, along roads, open fields

Range: throughout

Stan's Notes: A plant introduced from Eurasia and North Africa, the Crown Vetch was first planted here to stop erosion along roads after construction. It grows in very large masses, 25-35' (7.6-10.7 m) across, by stems that creep across the ground. When in flower, the large patches bloom into an impressive display of pink and white flowers. Once planted, the Crown Vetch is hard to remove. Like most members of the Pea or Bean family, Crown Vetch can fix nitrogen from the air into the soil, thus improving soil fertility.

CLUSTER TYPE	FLOWER TYPE	LEAF TYPE	LEAF ATTACHMENT	FRUIT
Round	**Irregular**	**Compound**	**Alternate**	**Pod**

PIPSISSEWA
Chimaphila umbellata

Family: Wintergreen (Pyrolaceae)

Size: 6-12" (15-30 cm)

Flower: a round cluster, 1-2" (2.5-5 cm) wide, of 3-7 waxy pink-to-white flowers; individual flowers, ½" (1 cm) wide, have 5 pointed petals; flowers sometimes hang down

Leaf: 2 or 3 tiers of whorled, shiny evergreen leaves, each whorl has 4-6 leaves; leaves are 1-3" (2.5-7.5 cm) long, with sharp teeth on the upper wider portion of the leaf

Bloom: summer

Cycle/Origin: perennial, native

Habitat: dry, shade, conifer woods

Range: eastern half of the state, mostly in the Arrowhead Region and BWCA

Stan's Notes: A small single-stemmed plant with whorled evergreen leaves, typically found growing under pine trees. The upper portion of the flower stalk is reddish pink, matching the color of the flowers. The genus name, *Chimaphila,* is Greek for *cheima* (winter) and *philein* (to love), which describes the evergreen leaves. The species name, *umbellata,* describes the umbrella-shaped flower cluster.

CLUSTER TYPE	FLOWER TYPE	LEAF TYPE	LEAF ATTACHMENT
Round	**Regular**	**Simple**	**Whorl**

PRAIRIE ONION
Allium stellatum

Family: Lily (Liliaceae)

Height: 1-2' (30-60 cm)

Flower: a round cluster, 1-2" (2.5-5 cm) wide, of many flowers that stand atop a single erect stem; individual flowers, ¼-½" (.6-1 cm) wide, are pink to rose with yellow centers

Leaf: a basal clump of thin grass-like leaves, ¼" (.6 cm) wide and up to 6" (15 cm) long; leaves often wither and die before flowers appear

Bloom: summer, fall

Cycle/Origin: perennial, native

Habitat: dry, sun, prairies, rocky soils

Range: throughout, except for the Arrowhead Region

Stan's Notes: All parts of the Prairie Onion, also called Wild Onion, have a strong onion fragrance. A true onion; it grows from a small papery bulb that was sometimes gathered for food. Do not pick or dig up this plant. The flower of the Prairie Onion always grows on erect stalks, distinguishing it from the Nodding Wild Onion. (*A. cernuum*), whose flowers always hang downward.

CLUSTER TYPE	FLOWER TYPE	LEAF TYPE	LEAF ATTACHMENT

Round	Regular	Simple	Basal

fruit

COMMON MILKWEED
Asclepias syriaca

Family: Milkweed (Asclepiadaceae)

Height: 2-5' (60-150 cm)

Flower: cream-colored, pink-tinged flowers, ½" (1 cm) wide, form a round cluster up to 2" (5 cm) wide; each flower has 5 downward-pointing petals and a 5-part pointed crown

Leaf: large, toothless, oval leaves, 4-6" (10-15 cm) long, bleed a white milky sap when broken

Fruit: elongated, green dry pods that split open to release many flat, brown seeds, each attached to hair-like fuzz that carries the seed away on the wind

Bloom: summer

Cycle/Origin: perennial, native

Habitat: wet or dry, sun or shade, fields

Range: throughout

Stan's Notes: There are over 2,000 milkweed species worldwide, 13 in Minnesota. A unique pollination system involves sacs of pollen that snag on an insect's leg; the insect then unwittingly inserts the sacs into slits on other flowers. The plant's milky sap contains cardiac glycosides and, if eaten, will cause hot flashes, rapid heart rate and general weakness. The Monarch butterfly lays its eggs exclusively on milkweeds. Monarch caterpillars ingest the toxic sap with no ill effects, but they then become toxic to birds and other animals. Fibers from old stems are used by orioles for making nests.

CLUSTER TYPE	FLOWER TYPE	LEAF TYPE	LEAF ATTACHMENT	FRUIT
		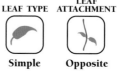		
Round	Irregular	Simple	Opposite	Pod

HEDGE NETTLE
Stachys palustris

Family: Mint (Lamiaceae)

Height: 1-2' (30-60 cm)

Flower: a single spike cluster, 2-3" (5-7.5 cm) long, of irregular pink flowers; individual flowers, ½-1" (1-2.5 cm) wide, have a pink upper hood and 3-lobed lower petals with dark purple spots and veins

Leaf: opposite lance-shaped leaves, 3-6" (7.5-15 cm) long, covered with coarse teeth and a deep network of veins; little or no leafstalk

Bloom: summer

Cycle/Origin: perennial, native

Habitat: wet, sun, along small lakes and streams, wet meadows and prairies

Range: throughout

Stan's Notes: Like most members of the Mint family, Hedge Nettle has a square stem with opposite leaves, but unlike others, it lacks a fragrance. Its single stem is covered with woolly hair. The Hedge Nettle's common name comes from its growing habitat along the edge (or hedge) of wetlands, growing in the same habitat as the Stinging Nettle. It is also called Common Woundwort because it was once used to help heal all types of wounds. Several types of Hedge Nettle grow in Minnesota.

CLUSTER TYPE	FLOWER TYPE	LEAF TYPE	LEAF ATTACHMENT
		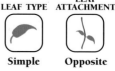	
Spike	Irregular	Simple	Opposite

PINK LADY'S SLIPPER
Cypripedium acaule

Family: Orchid (Orchidaceae)

Height: 6-15" (15-37.5 cm)

Flower: a single large pink flower, 2½" (6 cm) tall, per each leafless stalk; flowers are made up of an inflated lower petal (slipper) with red veins and a groove down the middle, along with 3 pointed and twisted greenish brown bracts (sepals)

Leaf: a pair of deep-veined basal leaves, up to 10" (25 cm) long, silvery beneath

Fruit: an erect pod-like container, 1-2" (2.5-5 cm) long

Bloom: spring, summer

Cycle/Origin: perennial, native

Habitat: dry, shade, conifer woods

Range: northern two-thirds of the state

Stan's Notes: Also called Moccasin Flower, Pink Lady's Slipper is found growing in dry pine forests and sometimes among rocky outcrops. One of the largest orchids in Minnesota, it produces only one flower per stalk (rarely, a second flower). Its flower is usually a deep rosy red (sometimes white) that becomes pale with age. Small bees enter the flower through a slit running the length of the lower inflated petal. Once inside, the bee can't back out and proceeds to the other side, picking up a pollen sac, which can then be deposited in the next orchid. Do not attempt to transplant.

FLOWER TYPE

Irregular

LEAF TYPE

Simple

LEAF ATTACHMENT

Basal

FRUIT

Pod

PINK PYROLA
Pyrola asarifolia

Family: Shinleaf (Pyrolaceae)

Size: 6-15" (15-37.5 cm)

Flower: a single, red-stemmed, spike cluster, 3-6" (7.5-15 cm) long, with up to 20 pink flowers; individual flowers, ¼-½" (.6-1 cm) wide, have 5 round petals, regular flowers, but often hang down to bell flowers

Leaf: round, dark green, evergreen basal leaves, 2-3" (5-7.5 cm) long, with red stalks

Fruit: a 5-chambered pod-like container

Bloom: summer

Cycle/Origin: perennial, native

Habitat: moist deciduous and conifer woods

Range: northern half of the state

Stan's Notes: A single, red-stemmed plant of moist woodlands, this is also called Shinleaf. There are six species of Pyrola in Minnesota. This is the only one with a pink flower; the rest are white-flowered. The thick, dark green leaves are evergreen. There are no leaves on the flower stalk. All the *Pyrola* species contain an aspirin-like substance. The leaves were made into a leaf plaster and used to treat wounds and reduce pain. The leaf plaster was called Shinplaster, resulting in its other common name. Often grows in a large group.

CLUSTER TYPE	FLOWER TYPE	LEAF TYPE	LEAF ATTACHMENT	FRUIT
		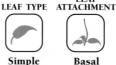		
Spike	Regular	Simple	Basal	Pod

PALE CORYDALIS
Corydalis sempervirens

Family: Poppy (Papaveraceae)

Size: 6-24" (15-60 cm)

Flower: a spike cluster, 3-6" (7.5-15 cm) long, of dangling pink and yellow tubular flowers; individual flowers, ½" (1 cm) long, are made up of 4 petals which form the pink tube; ends of petals have an upturned yellow lip

Leaf: pale blue green leaves, divided into many 3-lobed leaflets, ½" (1 cm) long

Fruit: thin, green pod-like container 1-2" (2.5-5 cm) long, turns brown when mature

Bloom: spring, summer

Cycle/Origin: perennial, native

Habitat: dry, sun, rock outcroppings

Range: northeastern half of the state, especially in the BWCA

Stan's Notes: A delicate herb of rocky outcroppings, Pale Corydalis is one of three species of *Corydalis* in Minnesota. Its pale blue green leaves and dangling pink and yellow flowers help to identify this plant of the North Country. Later in summer, the flowers produce thin, green seedpods that turn brown and release seeds when mature. *Corydalis* is Greek for "crested lark," referring to the shape of the flowers.

CLUSTER TYPE

Spike

FLOWER TYPE

Tube

LEAF TYPE

Compound

LEAF ATTACHMENT

Alternate

FRUIT

Pod

MOTHERWORT
Leonurus cardiaca

Family: Mint (Lamiaceae)

Height: 2-4' (60-120 cm)

Flower: spike clusters, 3-6" (7.5-15 cm) tall; individual flowers, pink-to-lilac and spine-tipped, ⅓" (.8 cm) long, arise near the stem at each leaf attachment (axil)

Leaf: sharp toothed opposite leaves, 2-4" (5-10 cm) long, with 3 pointed lobes

Bloom: summer

Cycle/Origin: perennial, non-native

Habitat: wet or dry, sun or shade, fields, disturbed soils, gardens

Range: throughout

Stan's Notes: A common plant of forgotten backyards or abandoned gardens, Motherwort originated in Asia and was imported from Europe. Its long history of medicinal use included cultivation to treat heart ailments; hence its species name, *cardiaca* (heart). The common name, "Motherwort," refers to its traditional use as a menstrual disorder treatment. Like other members of the Mint family, it has a square stem and opposite leaves. To identify, look for its three distinctive sharp-lobed leaves; the lower leaves have three lobes, while the upper leaves only have three sharp points in place of lobes.

CLUSTER TYPE	FLOWER TYPE	LEAF TYPE	LEAF ATTACHMENT
Spike	Irregular	Simple Lobed	Opposite

JOE-PYE WEED
Eupatoriadelphus maculatus

Family: Aster (Asteraceae)

Height: 2-10' (60-300 cm)

Flower: a large flat cluster, 5-10" (12.5-25 cm) wide, of pinkish purple flowers; hundreds of individual flowers, ¼" (.6 cm) wide, make up each flower head

Leaf: whorls of 3-5 coarsely toothed lance-shaped leaves, each 3-9" (7.5-22.5 cm) long

Bloom: summer

Cycle/Origin: perennial, native

Habitat: wet, sun, meadows, along roads, and streams

Range: throughout

Stan's Notes: Sometimes called Spotted Joe-pye Weed because its stem often has purplish spots. Joe-pye Weed is a very tall and robust plant that likes moist soil along streams and wet ditches. Its flowers are very attractive to many species of butterflies, and it makes a good garden plant (it can be purchased at many garden centers). One of several similar species of Joe-pye in Minnesota, all of which take their name from a medicine man named "Joe Pye." Like all members of the Aster family, Joe-pye Weed has a head of composite flowers made solely of disk flowers, lacking any ray flowers.

CLUSTER TYPE	FLOWER TYPE	LEAF TYPE	LEAF ATTACHMENT
Flat	Composite	Simple	Whorl

FIREWEED
Chamerion angustifolium

Family: Evening Primrose (Onagraceae)

Height: 2-6' (60-180 cm)

Flower: spike cluster, 6-12" (15-30 cm) long, with multiple pink flowers; individual flowers, 1" (2.5 cm) wide, made up of 4 oval petals; flowers open individually from the bottom of the spike up

Leaf: narrow, faintly toothed, willow-like leaves that grow up to 8" (20 cm) long

Fruit: slender, pod-like containers, up to 3" (7.5 cm) long, open from the top down to release silky down that carries the seeds away on the wind

Bloom: summer, fall

Cycle/Origin: perennial, native

Habitat: dry, shade, along roads, recently burned woodlands, conifer and deciduous woods

Range: northern two-thirds of the state

Stan's Notes: Also called Willow Herb because of its willow-shaped leaves, Fireweed is one of the first plants to grow after a forest fire, hence its common name. It grows individually in disturbed soils or in large masses after the wind has dispersed its seeds into burned areas. A very common wildflower found throughout the world, seven species of Fireweed make their home in Minnesota. A good nectar source for many species of butterflies.

CLUSTER TYPE	FLOWER TYPE	LEAF TYPE	LEAF ATTACHMENT	FRUIT
	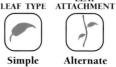			
Spike	**Regular**	**Simple**	**Alternate**	**Pod**

fruit

BITTERSWEET NIGHTSHADE
Solanum dulcamara

Family: Nightshade (Solanaceae)

Height: 2-8' (60-240 cm); vine

Flower: purple flowers, ½" (1 cm) wide, made up of 5 pointed and swept-back petals and resembling a purple (sometimes white) bursting star with a yellow center; its pointed center reminds some of a bird's beak

Leaf: toothless pointed leaves, 3½" (8.5 cm) long; most leaves have 2 small lobes at the base that do not always appear to be part of the main leaf

Fruit: shiny green berries ripen to shades of red

Bloom: spring, summer, fall

Cycle/Origin: perennial, non-native

Habitat: dry, sun and shade, disturbed areas

Range: throughout

Stan's Notes: A weak vine that was introduced into North America from Eurasia, Bittersweet Nightshade is easily identified by its dark purple flowers with yellow centers as well as its rich red berries. It is sometimes called Deadly Nightshade because its leaves and unripe fruit contain the alkaloid solanine. Although the toxin is not fatal, it can cause problems for young children if eaten in any quantity. Closely related to the common garden tomato, this wildflower was dubbed "Bittersweet" because of the taste of its leaves.

FLOWER TYPE	LEAF TYPE	LEAF ATTACHMENT	FRUIT
Regular	Simple Lobed	Alternate	Berry

CHEESES
Malva neglecta

Family: Mallow (Malvaceae)

Height: 6-12" (15-30 cm)

Flower: up to 20 lavender-to-white flowers, ½" (1 cm) wide, made up of 5 petals notched at the tip; flowers are located down low near the main stem where each leaf is attached (axis)

Leaf: nearly round, toothed leaves, 1½" (4 cm) wide, with 5 lobes and deep veining

Fruit: round segmented pod

Bloom: spring, summer, fall

Cycle/Origin: annual, non-native

Habitat: dry, sun, barnyards, disturbed soils, along sidewalks, gardens

Range: throughout

Stan's Notes: Also called Common Mallow or Cheeseweed, Cheeses is a common barnyard plant introduced from Eurasia and North Africa. Its flowers resemble those of Hollyhocks, a common garden plant from the same family. The common name, "Cheeses," comes from its round, segmented fruit pod, which looks like a wheel of cheese. The species name, *neglecta*, refers to the plant's habit of growing in neglected gardens. It is a host plant for Painted Lady and Checkered Skipper butterfly caterpillars.

FLOWER TYPE	LEAF TYPE	LEAF ATTACHMENT	FRUIT
	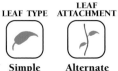		
Regular	Simple	Alternate	Pod

DAME'S ROCKET
Hesperis matronalis

Family: Mustard (Brassicaceae)

Height: 1-3' (30-90 cm)

Flower: a purple, blue or white flower, ½-1" (1-2.5 cm) wide, with 4 round petals; flower stalks are crowded with flowers and bloom from the bottom up

Leaf: wide, coarsely toothed, lance-shaped leaves, 1-3" (2.5-7.5 cm) long, with short leafstalks; both stems and leaves are covered with fine hairs

Fruit: thin, wiry seedpods, ½-3" (1-7.5 cm) long, that split open lengthwise to release tiny black seeds

Bloom: spring, summer

Cycle/Origin: annual or biennial, non-native

Habitat: wet or dry, sun or shade, along roads, open fields, near old homesteads

Range: throughout

Stan's Notes: Now well established in Minnesota, Dame's Rocket, a European native, is a garden escapee that closely resembles Wild Blue Phlox (pg. 47) or garden phlox. Phlox have five petals while Dame's Rocket has only four, as do all members of the Mustard family. Also called Sweet Rocket or Dame's Violet, this usually grows as an annual or biennial; rarely as a perennial. If its flower heads are cut back, it will bloom a second time. Flowers attract nectaring butterflies, (especially Tiger Swallowtails), moths and hummingbirds.

FLOWER TYPE	LEAF TYPE	LEAF ATTACHMENT	FRUIT
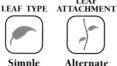			
Regular	Simple	Alternate	Pod

SHOOTING STAR
Dodecatheon radicatum

Family: Primrose (Primulaceae)

Height: 10-20" (25-50 cm)

Flower: each plant has only 1 stalk, producing 1-5 nodding purple flowers, 1" (2.5 cm) wide; individual flowers each have 5 backward-curved, purple petals with yellow centers

Leaf: toothless, lance-shaped basal leaves, up to 6" (15 cm) long, with round tips

Bloom: spring

Cycle/Origin: perennial, native

Habitat: dry, sun or shade, deciduous wood, prairies

Range: southeastern corner of the state

Stan's Notes: A common prairie spring wildflower, Shooting Star was called "Prairie Pointers" by early prairie settlers. The pointed center of the flower is made up of united stamens, an arrangement that makes insects force their tongues between the stamens to sip nectar. The flowers grow downward, but the flower stalk becomes upright after pollination. Often grown in gardens, Shooting Star's common name comes from its star-shaped flower that arches at the top of a long, thin "shooting" stem.

FLOWER TYPE	LEAF TYPE	LEAF ATTACHMENT
Regular	Simple	Basal

SHOWY ORCHIS
Galearis spectabilis

Family: Orchid (Orchidaceae)

Height: 5-12" (12.5-30 cm)

Flower: 12-20 spectacular, two-toned flowers, 1" (2.5 cm) tall, each made up of 2 petals and 3 petal-like sepals that fuse together to form a purplish pink hood that hangs over white lower petals; several flowers grow along a single thick stem

Leaf: 2 long basal leaves, 10" (25 cm) long and up to 3" (7.5 cm) wide, with deeply ribbed parallel veins clasp the stem; flower stem has several smaller lance-shaped leaves, 1-3" (2.5-7.5 cm) long

Bloom: spring

Cycle/Origin: perennial, native

Habitat: wet, sun, swamps, moist woods

Range: southern half of the state, except for the southwestern corner

Stan's Notes: A woodland species of orchid with a pleasant fragrance. Unlike the Showy Lady's Slipper (pg. 273), this orchid has a colored hood over a white lower petal. Lower white petal (lip) is a landing platform for pollinating insects that must push hard to get inside. This plant is erratic in its presence in that it may bloom for several years and then disappear or show up some distance away. Many orchids take up to 15 years to mature and produce flowers. Enjoy these flowers in the wild and don't dig them up.

FLOWER TYPE	LEAF TYPE	LEAF ATTACHMENT	LEAF ATTACHMENT	LEAF ATTACHMENT
Irregular	Simple	Alternate	Basal	Clasping

SPOTTED KNAPWEED
Centaurea stoebe

Family: Aster (Asteraceae)

Height: 2-3' (60-90 cm)

Flower: each plant produces 25-100 lavender-to-purple flower heads, 1" (2.5 cm) wide, made entirely of disk flowers; each flower is surrounded underneath by a black-tipped, brown, prickly bract

Leaf: deeply lobed lower leaves, 4-8" (10-20 cm) long, with many narrow lobes; upper leaves (also deeply lobed) are much smaller, 1-2" (2.5-5 cm) long, with very narrow pointed lobes

Bloom: summer, fall

Cycle/Origin: biennial, non-native

Habitat: dry, sun, fields, along roads

Range: throughout

Stan's Notes: Spotted Knapweed is a non-native plant commonly found growing in large groups along the side of the road and in open fields. It looks a lot like the garden annual, Bachelor Button. Its lavender flowers can range from white to red, but always have the brown triangular bracts. Its leaves often appear wilted and curled, and it is considered a noxious weed by many state agricultural departments because of its aggressiveness in crowding out other plants. Possibly an allelopathic plant that chemically changes the soil so as to discourage other plants and favor its own offspring.

FLOWER TYPE	LEAF TYPE	LEAF ATTACHMENT
Composite	Simple Lobed	Alternate

WILD BERGAMOT
Monarda fistulosa

Family: Mint (Lamiaceae)

Height: 2-4' (60-120 cm)

Flower: a round cluster, 1-2" (2.5-5 cm) wide, of many individual pale lavender flowers; individual flowers, ¼" (.6 cm) long, are tubular with a lower curved petal and a thin straight petal

Leaf: coarsely toothed, lance shaped leaves, 1-3" (2.5-7.5 cm) long, grow on short leafstalks

Bloom: summer

Cycle/Origin: perennial, native

Habitat: dry, sun, fields, prairies, along roads

Range: throughout

Stan's Notes: Also called Horsemint or Bee Balm, Wild Bergamot is a tall single-stemmed plant of open fields and prairies. The heads of its lavender flowers attract many insects, including bees, butterflies and beetles. Look for its square stems and opposite pairs of leaves to help identify this member of the Mint family. The entire plant has a strong odor when rubbed or crushed, and it has been used in folk medicine as a "mint tea" to treat many respiratory and digestive ailments. The common name, "Bergamot," refers to a small citrus tree that produces a similar odor. This mint's oil is an essential flavoring ingredient in Earl Grey tea.

CLUSTER TYPE	LEAF TYPE	LEAF ATTACHMENT
Round	Simple	Opposite

Purple Prairie Clover
Dalea purpureum

Family: Pea or Bean (Fabaceae)

Height: 1-3' (30-90 cm)

Flower: tiny, 5-petaled, purple flowers, ⅙" (.5 cm) long, cluster to form a thick, thimble-shaped flower head, 1-2" (2.5-5 cm) tall spike

Leaf: small leaves, ½-¾" (1-2 cm) long, with 5-7 narrow leaflets

Bloom: summer, fall

Cycle/Origin: perennial, native

Habitat: dry, sun, prairies, along old railroad beds

Range: throughout

Stan's Notes: Purple Prairie Clover often grows in large clumps, creating a spectacular sight when in bloom. Vivid bluish purple flowers bloom from the bottom up on the thimble or cone-like head. This member of the Pea or Bean family lacks the typical pea flower, and has the ability to gather nitrogen from the air and trap it in the soil, thus enhancing soil fertility. Also called Prairie Clover, Purple Prairie Clover is similar to a white species, *D. candida* (pg. 261), which has taller cones and very different leaves. Host plant for the Dog Face butterfly and some of the blues butterfly caterpillars.

CLUSTER TYPE	LEAF TYPE	LEAF ATTACHMENT
Spike	Compound	Alternate

NEW ENGLAND ASTER
Symphyotrichum novae-angliae

Family: Aster (Asteraceae)

Height: 3-7' (90-210 cm)

Flower: many (25-100) bright purple and yellow flowers per plant; individual flower heads, 1-2" (2.5-5 cm) wide, have 35-45 purple petals (ray flowers) with a yellow center (disk flowers); flower stalks are covered with sticky hairs

Leaf: many long, toothless, stalkless lance-shaped leaves, 1-5" (2.5-12.5 cm) long, that clasp the stem; leaves are large near the base and extremely small near the flowers

Bloom: fall

Cycle/Origin: perennial, native

Habitat: moist, sun, prairies, along roads

Range: throughout, except for the Arrowhead Region

Stan's Notes: A large, showy, autumn-flowering plant, New England Aster features highly variable flower color, ranging from pink to lavender or from blue to white, although it usually presents a rich purple. Its stems are often hairy and crowded with clasping leaves; leaves near the ground fall off early, leaving "naked legs." It is often grown in gardens. A great nectar plant for its long bloom time in autumn. Heavily visited by migrating Monarch butterflies.

FLOWER TYPE	LEAF TYPE	LEAF ATTACHMENT	LEAF ATTACHMENT
Composite	**Simple**	**Alternate**	**Clasping**

139

WILD GERANIUM
Geranium maculatum

Family: Geranium (Geraniaceae)

Height: 1-2' (30-60 cm)

Flower: group of 2-10 regular lavender flowers; individual flowers, 1-2" (2.5-5 cm) wide, are made up of 5 heavily veined lavender petals

Leaf: basal leaves, 4-5" (10-12.5 cm) long, on long stalks; leaves are coarsely toothed and deeply veined with 5-7 elongated lobes; only 2-3 stem leaves (cauline) per plant

Fruit: elongated, beak-like, pod-like container that splits lengthwise to release many seeds

Bloom: spring

Cycle/Origin: perennial, native

Habitat: dry, shade, deciduous woods, meadows

Range: throughout

Stan's Notes: A common spring-blooming perennial of shady deciduous woodlands. The Wild Geranium's delicate lavender flowers rise above its many-lobed leaves. Its seed capsules split into five long and curled "peals" to release seeds. Its genus name, *Geranium*, comes from the Greek *geranos*, or (a crane), and describes its seed capsule's long narrow shape like that of the bill of a crane. It is also called Crane's-bill Geranium.

FLOWER TYPE

Regular

LEAF TYPE

Simple Lobed

LEAF ATTACHMENT

Basal

LEAF ATTACHMENT

Opposite

FRUIT

Pod

FIELD THISTLE
Cirsium discolor

Family: Aster (Asteraceae)

Height: 3-5' (90-150 cm)

Flower: pale purple flower heads, 2" (5 cm) wide, with a large, green, spiny base; each flower head (5-20 per plant) is closely clasped by a set of leaves (bracts)

Leaf: elongated, spine-tipped, lobed leaves, 6-12" (15-30 cm) long, clasp the stem; the underside of each leaf is densely covered with white hairs

Bloom: summer

Cycle/Origin: perennial, native

Habitat: dry, sun, open fields, along roads

Range: throughout

Stan's Notes: The white "wool" under its clasping leaves and the set of small leaves just beneath each flower help to positively identify the Field Thistle, one of many thistles found in Minnesota. Each plant produces many pale purple flower heads on only a few stalks. The plant is a favorite of bees and wasps, who sip nectar and in turn pollinate the flower. A good nectar plant for attracting Tiger Swallowtails and Monarch butterflies. Often confused with Bull Thistle (pg. 169), but the Field Thistle leaves are not nearly as prickly and its flower is much paler.

FLOWER TYPE	LEAF TYPE	LEAF ATTACHMENT	LEAF ATTACHMENT
Composite	**Simple Lobed**	**Alternate**	**Clasping**

HOARY VERVAIN
Verbena stricta

Family: Vervain (Verbenaceae)

Height: 1-3' (30-90 cm)

Flower: usually a single spike, 2-5" (5-12.5 cm) long, of purple-to-blue tube-like flowers, ½" (1 cm) long, but it can have multiple flower stalks; each flower is made up of 5 fused petals

Leaf: oval leaves, 2-3" (5-7.5 cm) long, are thick and covered with dense whitish hairs; they lack a leaf-stalk but do not actually clasp its square stem

Bloom: summer

Cycle/Origin: perennial, native

Habitat: dry, fields, along ditches, shores, roadsides

Range: southern two-thirds of the state

Stan's Notes: Hoary Vervain is a tall slender plant, sometimes with multiple, pencil-thin flower spikes that bloom from the bottom up. Its stems are square with opposite leaves, which is why it is often confused with a member of the Mint family. The genus name, *Verbena,* is Latin for "sacred plant," and refers to an ancient time when the plant was thought to have medicinal properties. Its flowers can be rosy but are usually more purple than the blue flowers of the Blue Vervain (pg. 49).

CLUSTER TYPE

Spike

LEAF TYPE

Simple

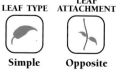

LEAF ATTACHMENT

Opposite

145

PURPLE CONEFLOWER
Echinacea purpurea

Family: Aster (Asteraceae)

Height: 2-3' (60-90 cm)

Flower: large flower heads, 3-5" (7.5-12.5 cm) wide, made up of 14-20 droopy purple-to-blue (sometimes white) petals (ray flowers) that surround a cone-shaped, spiny, orange center (disk flowers)

Leaf: coarsely toothed, 3-veined leaves, 5" (12.5 cm) wide and up to 8" (20 cm) long; leaves are rough to the touch because of many small hairs

Bloom: summer, fall

Cycle/Origin: perennial, native

Habitat: dry, sun, prairies, along roads, ditches

Range: throughout, mainly in the western half of the state

Stan's Notes: A tall showy flower of the prairies, Purple Coneflower is a popular plant for herbal remedies. Its leaves and stems are rough to touch because of stiff hairs covering the plant. The American Goldfinch finds its seed heads irresistible, and the plant is also a favorite of many butterfly species that visit to sip nectar.

FLOWER TYPE	LEAF TYPE	LEAF ATTACHMENT
Composite	**Simple**	**Alternate**

PURPLE FRINGED ORCHID
Habenaria psycodes

Family: Orchid (Orchidaceae)

Height: 1-2' (30-60 cm)

Flower: a thick spike, 6-10" (15-25 cm) long, of many lavender-to-purple flowers, ½-1" (1-2.5 cm) wide, each made up of 1 upper petal and 3 lower petals with many fine notches that form a fringe

Leaf: linear tulip-like leaves, up to 8" (20 cm) long, stand erect from the base; thinner, parallel-veined stem leaves, up to 4" (10 cm) long, clasp the stem

Bloom: summer

Cycle/Origin: perennial, native

Habitat: wet, sun, grassy marshes, damp woodland borders, prairies

Range: eastern half of the state

Stan's Notes: The genus name, *Habenaria*, is Latin for "rein" and refers to the long spur at the base of each flower petal ("fringed" refers to the petal edge). Its flowers are pollinated when moths insert their tongues into a flower and emerge with a sticky pollen sack (pollinia) that they unwittingly carry to another flower. This is one of about ten species of "rein" orchids in Minnesota. It has a specific mycorrhizal relationship which so far has not been cultivated; thus it won't grow in a garden. It should never be picked or transplanted. Enjoy this flower with your eyes and camera only.

CLUSTER TYPE	FLOWER TYPE	LEAF TYPE	LEAF ATTACHMENT	LEAF ATTACHMENT	LEAF ATTACHMENT

Spike	**Irregular**	**Simple**	**Alternate**	**Basal**	**Clasping**

ROUGH BLAZING STAR
Liatris aspera

Family: Aster (Asteraceae)

Height: 16-48" (40-120 cm)

Flower: a single tall stem, 6-12" (15-30 cm) long, of many round, purple flower heads, each ¾" (2 cm) wide, and made up of 25-40 florets (disk flowers); both stalkless and stalked flower heads occur on 1 stem, and each flower head is surrounded by flat rounded bracts

Leaf: thin lance-shaped leaves, ¼" (.6 cm) wide and 4-12" (10-30 cm) long, alternate along the stem; upper leaves become progressively smaller near the top

Bloom: summer, fall

Cycle/Origin: perennial, native

Habitat: dry, sun, sandy soils, prairies

Range: throughout, except for the Arrowhead Region

Stan's Notes: One of many Blazing Star species in Minnesota, Rough Blazing Star is distinguished by its round, flat flower bracts and its rough feel (the species name, *aspera*, is Latin for "rough"). A plant of the native tall-grass prairies, Rough Blazing Star is relished by deer and cattle. Its flowers have distinct spaces between each flower head. This plant is a major nectar source for fall-migrating Monarch butterflies. Unlike many other floral spikes, its flowers bloom from the top to the bottom of the spike over time.

CLUSTER TYPE	FLOWER TYPE	LEAF TYPE	LEAF ATTACHMENT
			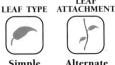
Spike	Composite	Simple	Alternate

PRAIRIE BLAZING STAR
Liatris pycnostachya

Family: Aster (Asteraceae)

Height: 2-5' (60-150 cm)

Flower: a spike cluster, 6-18" (15-45 cm) long, made of many purple, round flower heads, ½" (1 cm) long, crowded together along a main stem giving an appearance of one long compact flower; individual flowers are composed of 8-10 florets (disk flowers); florets are surrounded by pointed, backward-bent bracts

Leaf: lower, grass-like leaves up to 12" (30 cm) long and ½" (1 cm) wide, alternate along the single hairy stem; leaves become progressively smaller near the top

Bloom: summer

Cycle/Origin: perennial, native

Habitat: wet, sun, sandy soils, moist areas in prairies

Range: throughout, except for the Arrowhead Region

Stan's Notes: One of Minnesota's many Blazing Star species, the Latin name, *pycnostachya*, means "crowded," describing both its leaves and flowers. A very showy plant of the native tall-grass prairie habitat, Prairie Blazing Star is relished by deer and cattle. Look for its hairy stems and leaves. A great nectar source for butterflies, it blooms about three weeks earlier than Rough Blazing Star (pg. 151). Look for it in your local garden center, where it is sold as a garden perennial. Also called Tall Blazing Star or Prairie Gayfeather.

CLUSTER TYPE	FLOWER TYPE	LEAF TYPE	LEAF ATTACHMENT
			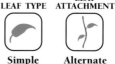
Spike	Composite	Simple	Alternate

PURPLE LOOSESTRIFE
Lythrum salicaria

Family: Loosestrife (Lythraceae)

Height: 2-5' (60-150 cm)

Flower: a long spike cluster, 1-2' (30-60 cm), of purple flowers; each flower, ½-¾" (1-2 cm) wide, is made up of 4-6 petals, rising on short stalks near the leaf attachment

Leaf: mostly opposite, but often whorled in 3s and 4s, narrow lance-shaped leaves, 1-4" (2.5-10 cm) long; leaves nearly clasp the stem and are smaller near the top

Bloom: summer

Cycle/Origin: perennial, non-native

Habitat: wet, sun, quiet waters, ponds, marshes, swamps

Range: throughout

Stan's Notes: A very showy plant that often grows in large numbers, Purple Loosestrife puts on an impressive show in bloom. One of the few plants that has both opposite and whorled leaves on the same plant, it was once grown as a garden plant because of its striking magenta flower spikes. This native of Eurasia is often considered a noxious weed because it takes over and pushes out native plants, such as cattails and bulrush. Efforts are under way to reduce the loosestrife population by releasing special beetles that feed on the plant's roots and leaves.

CLUSTER TYPE	FLOWER TYPE	LEAF TYPE	LEAF ATTACHMENT	LEAF ATTACHMENT
			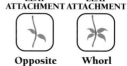	
Spike	**Regular**	**Simple**	**Opposite**	**Whorl**

seed

PRAIRIE SMOKE
Geum triflorum

Family: Rose (Rosaceae)

Height: 6-16" (15-40 cm)

Flower: groups of 3 or 6 droopy, reddish brown, bell-shaped flowers, ¾" (2 cm) long, grow on each stalk; each flower has 5 pointed petal-like sepals that alternate with narrow bracts and 5 very small white-to-pinkish petals

Leaf: long basal leaves, 4-9" (10-22.5 cm) long; divided into many small-toothed leaflets

Bloom: spring

Cycle/Origin: perennial, native

Habitat: dry, sun, prairies

Range: throughout, except for the Arrowhead Region

Stan's Notes: Also called Purple Avens, this is a common plant of native prairies and a favorite of poets and photographers because of its seed head of 2" (5 cm) feathery plumes (some say it looks like a feather duster) waving in the wind, giving a "smoky" appearance. Its bell-shaped flowers hang down, but after pollination the stem straightens up and the seed head stands erect. One of the first blooming in the native prairie, Prairie Smoke takes its name both from its natural environment and the "smoky" appearance of its seed heads.

FLOWER TYPE	LEAF TYPE	LEAF ATTACHMENT
Bell	**Compound**	**Basal**

SPOTTED CORALROOT
Corallorhiza maculata

Family: Orchid (Orchidaceae)

Height: 6-20" (15-50 cm)

Flower: a single, leafless, red stem produces 20-40 red, yellow and white flowers, ¾" (2 cm) tall; each flower is made up of 5 petal-like sepals that surround a white lower petal (lip) with purple spots

Leaf: no leaves; tubular sheaths up to 3" (7.5 cm) long

Fruit: nodding pod-like container, 1" (2.5 cm) long

Bloom: summer

Cycle/Origin: perennial, native

Habitat: wet, shade, conifer woods

Range: throughout, except for the southwestern corner

Stan's Notes: An unusual orchid of the northern woods, Spotted Coralroot is often described as a leafless red stalk with many flowers. It usually grows in groups of up to ten stems. It lacks chlorophyll, and is instead nourished through a partnership with an underground fungus (mycorrhiza) that breaks down dead organic matter (saprophytic) for the plant to feed on. Since it doesn't make food from sunlight, this orchid lacks traditional leaves, and instead has only sheaths. One of four species of coral orchid in Minnesota, its common name comes from its coral-shaped roots. Please don't pick or try to transplant. It won't grow in gardens.

CLUSTER TYPE

Spike

FLOWER TYPE

Irregular

FRUIT

Pod

SWAMP LAUREL
Kalmia polifolia

Family: Heath (Ericaceae)

Height: 1-3' (30-90 cm); shrub

Flower: rosy red, cup-shaped flowers, ¾-1" (2-2.5 cm) wide, cluster near the top of woody stalks; 5 petals fuse to form the cup shape, and each flower has a very long protruding center

Leaf: leathery evergreen leaves, 1-2" (2.5-5 cm) long, grow opposite along a stem with 2 edges; each leaf is just ¼" (.6 cm) wide, and its edges (margins) roll under; no hair underneath leaf

Bloom: spring

Cycle/Origin: perennial, native

Habitat: wet, sun, bogs

Range: northern half of the state, especially in the Arrowhead Region and BWCA

Stan's Notes: A woody shrub of wet bogs, Swamp Laurel's stems have two edges and are light tan or gray in color. Its leaves, twigs and flowers are poisonous, so it's important not to confuse it with edible Labrador Tea (pg. 281), which has dense brown hairs underneath. Swamp Laurel has no hairs. The genus name, *Kalmia*, honors the Swedish botanist Peter Kalm.

FLOWER TYPE

Regular

LEAF TYPE

Simple

LEAF ATTACHMENT

Opposite

RED CLOVER
Trifolium pratense

Family: Pea or Bean (Fabaceae)

Height: 6-24" (15-60 cm)

Flower: round clusters of 50-100 rosy red flowers, ⅛-¼" (.3-.6 cm) long, that appear as 1 large red flower, 1" (2.5 cm) wide

Leaf: typical clover leaf, ½-2" (1-5 cm) wide; made up of 3 leaflets; each leaflet has white markings in a V-shape (chevron)

Bloom: spring, summer, fall

Cycle/Origin: perennial, non-native

Habitat: wet or dry, sun, old fields, pastures

Range: throughout

Stan's Notes: A native of Europe, Red Clover was introduced to North America as a hay and pasture crop. It has since escaped to the wild and is now one of the most common roadside plants. It is still grown as a rotation crop to improve the soil fertility because its roots fix nitrogen into the soil. The genus name, *Trifolium*, means "three leaves," which describes the three leaflets, while the species name, *pratense*, means "meadows" and refers to where you find it growing. Pollinated nearly exclusively by Honeybees. Without these insects, it is unable to produce seeds and will eventually die out. Seeds can lay dormant for years before sprouting.

CLUSTER TYPE
Round

FLOWER TYPE
Irregular

LEAF TYPE
Compound

LEAF ATTACHMENT
Alternate

INDIAN PAINTBRUSH
Castilleja coccinea

Family: Snapdragon (Scrophulariaceae)

Height: 1-2' (30-60 cm)

Flower: inconspicuous greenish yellow flowers, 1" (2.5 cm) long, interspersed among a cluster of bright, 3-lobed, red-tipped, leafy bracts that are often mistaken for the flower petals

Leaf: single hairy stem; nearly clasping alternate leaves usually divided into 3 narrow, finger-like lobes

Fruit: small, pod-like container, ¾" (2 cm) long, contains many brown seeds

Bloom: spring, summer

Cycle/Origin: annual, native

Habitat: moist, open fields, prairies, rocky outcroppings

Range: throughout, except for the southwestern corner

Stan's Notes: This plant is so named because each stem is topped with scarlet, resembling a painter's brush. A member of the Snapdragon family, it is also called Painted Cup due to its vermilion cup-shaped bracts. Thought to be semiparasitic, its roots tap into those of other plants to gain nutrients. This most colorful of Minnesota wildflowers is also found in a less common yellow variety and is one of about 110 species of paintbrush in North America. Only a few species occur in the eastern half of the U.S. Legend has it that it sprang up where an Indian discarded his brushes after painting a scarlet sunset.

FLOWER TYPE

Tube

LEAF TYPE

Simple Lobed

LEAF ATTACHMENT

Alternate

FRUIT

Pod

fruit

COLUMBINE
Aquilegia canadensis

Family: Buttercup (Ranunculaceae)

Height: 1-2' (30-60 cm)

Flower: a collection of 5 upside-down red orange tubes forms a bell, 1-2" (2.5-5 cm) long, with yellow tips and hollow nectar-filled spurs

Leaf: long-stalked leaves, 4-6" (10-15 cm) long, divided into 9-27 thin, light green leaflets; each leaflet has 3 lobes

Fruit: papery pod-like container that splits along its side to release many shiny round seeds

Bloom: spring, summer

Cycle/Origin: perennial, native

Habitat: dry, rocky places, open deciduous woods, shade

Range: throughout

Stan's Notes: Children often mistake the Columbine for Honeysuckle and bite off its long spurs to suck out the nectar. While there is only one native species in Minnesota, numerous cultivated species have escaped into the wild. This plant was once considered for our national wildflower because its flower resembles the Bald Eagle's talons; *Aquilegia* is Latin for "eagle." Its nectar tubes make it a favorite flower of hummingbirds and long-tongued moths; some insects chew holes in its tubes, cheating to get a little nectar. Grows well in a garden. Collect only seeds; don't dig up the plant.

FLOWER TYPE	LEAF TYPE	LEAF ATTACHMENT	FRUIT
Bell	**Compound**	**Alternate**	**Pod**

BULL THISTLE
Cirsium vulgare

Family: Aster (Asteraceae)

Height: 2-6' (60-180 cm)

Flower: large, reddish purple flower heads, 1½-2" (4-5 cm) wide, sit on a wide green base that narrows near its center; 1 to several flower heads per stem

Leaf: narrow leaves, 3-6" (7.5-15 cm) long, with many lobes, each ending in a sharp spine

Bloom: summer, fall

Cycle/Origin: biennial, non-native

Habitat: dry, open fields, sun, disturbed soils

Range: throughout

Stan's Notes: The spiniest of the many different thistle species found in Minnesota, the Bull Thistle is a true biennial, producing a low rosette of leaves its first year and sending up a tall flower stalk in the second. A favorite flower of large bees, the Bull Thistle's little seeds feature tiny, parachute-like thistledown to carry them off on the winds after pollination. The seeds are a favorite food of American Goldfinches, which use the thistledown to line their nests and, therefore, must wait until late summer to raise their young. Often confused with Field Thistle (pg. 143), Bull Thistle has a much deeper reddish purple flower and more spines on its leaves.

FLOWER TYPE

Composite

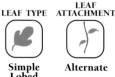

LEAF TYPE

Simple Lobed

LEAF ATTACHMENT

Alternate

flower

PITCHER PLANT
Sarracenia purpurea

Family: Pitcher Plant (Sarraceniaceae)

Height: 8-24" (20-60 cm)

Flower: a large, maroon-to-deep red, bell-shaped flower, 2-3" (5-7.5 cm) wide, droops from a single, tall, leafless stalk; 5 petals and 5 petal-like sepals form the bell shape

Leaf: a single stalkless leaf forms a long hollow tube to hold rainwater with a large lip on its upper edge

Fruit: round pod-like capsule containing seeds

Bloom: summer

Cycle/Origin: perennial, native

Habitat: wet, bogs

Range: northeastern two-thirds of the state

Stan's Notes: A water plant of acid bogs, the Pitcher Plant relies on insects rather than soil to gain its nutrients. Its leaves form a tall tube or funnel that fills with rainwater, and downward-pointing hairs line the opening of the tube. This allows insects to travel down but not up; unsuspecting bugs are thereby captured. The plant secretes enzymes into the rainwater, which helps it to digest any insect that falls into the watery trap. The plant then absorbs the nutrients, especially nitrogen, which is otherwise nearly inaccessible in bog soils because of the high acidity.

FLOWER TYPE	LEAF TYPE	LEAF ATTACHMENT	FRUIT
Bell	Simple	Basal	Pod

fruit

SWAMP MILKWEED
Asclepias incarnata

Family: Milkweed (Asclepiadaceae)

Height: 1-4' (30-120 cm)

Flower: rosy red-and-white flowers, ¼" (.6 cm) wide, form several flat clusters, 2-3" (5-7.5 cm) wide; individual flowers have 5 downward-curving petals and 5 upward petals, resembling a crown

Leaf: narrow opposite leaves, ½" (1 cm) wide, and up to 4" (10 cm) long; short leafstalk and no teeth

Fruit: elongated narrow pod, 2-4" (5-10 cm) long, opens along one side to release 10-20 brown, disk-shaped seeds, each with white tuft

Bloom: summer

Cycle/Origin: perennial, native

Habitat: wet, sun, swamps, streams, wet meadows

Range: throughout

Stan's Notes: This plant usually has one long stem that branches near the top into several flat-topped flower clusters. Its upper stems often turn rosy red, matching its flowers. Each flower has a slit allowing an insect's legs to slip inside and emerge with a pair of pollen sacs that will pollinate another flower. So, only a few flowers become pollinated. This milkweed has less milky sap than others, but it has been used in folk medicine for a variety of ailments. A host and nectar plant for Monarchs and a good plant for a butterfly garden.

CLUSTER TYPE	FLOWER TYPE	LEAF TYPE	LEAF ATTACHMENT	FRUIT

Flat	Irregular	Simple	Opposite	Pod

CARDINAL FLOWER
Lobelia cardinalis

Family: Bellflower (Campanulaceae)

Height: 2-4' (60-120 cm)

Flower: a tall open spike, 1-2' (30-60 cm) long, of scarlet red flowers, 1½" (4 cm) wide, that alternate on a stem, with the bottom flowers opening before the upper; 5 narrow petals, 2 upper and 3 spreading lower, unite to form a thin tube at its base

Leaf: toothed, lance-shaped leaves, up to 6" (15 cm) long, nearly clasp the stem

Bloom: summer, fall

Cycle/Origin: perennial, native

Habitat: wet, shade, along streams and wetlands, swamps

Range: southeastern corner of the state along waterways

Stan's Notes: By far one of the most spectacular wildflowers of Minnesota, the Cardinal Flower is found growing in small patches along southeastern Minnesota's streams and rivers. These flowers can be grown in gardens, but its roots need to be wet and its flowers must have some sunlight. The Cardinal Flower is not very successful at reproducing, perhaps because it can only be pollinated by hummingbirds. Do not dig this plant from the wild (it can be purchased at garden centers). While it occasionally produces white or rose-colored blooms, its scarlet red flowers resemble the bright red robes worn by Roman Catholic cardinals, thus providing its common name.

CLUSTER TYPE

Spike

FLOWER TYPE

Irregular

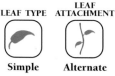

LEAF TYPE

Simple

LEAF ATTACHMENT

Alternate

COMMON CHICKWEED
Stellaria media

Family: Pink (Caryophyllaceae)

Height: 3-9" (7.5-22.5 cm)

Flower: star-shaped, 5-petaled, white flowers, ¼" (.6 cm) wide, found singly at the end of a tiny stalk; each petal is deeply divided, giving the appearance of 2 petals and making the flower look as though it actually has 10 petals

Leaf: small, simple, toothless pointed leaves, ½-1" (1-2.5 cm) long, sit opposite one other on the stem; the upper leaves clasp the stem, while the lower leaves attach by short thin stalks that are often covered with tiny hairs

Bloom: spring, summer, fall

Cycle/Origin: annual, non-native

Habitat: wet or dry, sun or shade, a plant of gardens and especially lawns or disturbed soil

Range: throughout

Stan's Notes: A common weak-stemmed plant that lays across the ground in large mats, the Common Chickweed displays many flowers per plant and when open, its white flowers look like a sky full of tiny stars. Gardeners are often pestered by the prodigious growth of this annual, which is easily pulled out of the ground. One of seven species of chickweed in Minnesota, the Common Chickweed is the only non-native and the most widespread.

FLOWER TYPE	LEAF TYPE	LEAF ATTACHMENT
Regular	Simple	Opposite

fruit

BEARBERRY
Arctostaphylos uva-ursi

Family: Heath (Ericaceae)

Size: 6-12" (15-30 cm)

Flower: a round cluster, 1" (2.5 cm) wide, of white-to-pink, bell-shaped flowers; individual flowers, ¼" (.6 cm) long, are waxy white bell flowers tinged with pink at the narrow flower opening

Leaf: oval-shaped, smooth, leathery leaves without teeth attach alternately along the creeping woody stem

Fruit: cluster of bright red berries

Bloom: spring, summer

Cycle/Origin: perennial, native

Habitat: dry, sun, exposed rocky sites in conifer forests, especially in the BWCA

Range: throughout, except for the extreme south and west portions of the state

Stan's Notes: A woody shrub, appearing more like herbaceous ground cover, Bearberry's woody stems are usually hidden under moss or leaf litter. The woody stems have a papery bark that sloughs off (exfoliates). Often forms large mats near campsites and along portages in the BWCA. The red berries are eaten by many birds and especially bears. The genus name comes from the Greek *arctos* (bear) and *staphyle* (bunch of grapes), describing the fruit.

CLUSTER TYPE	FLOWER TYPE	LEAF TYPE	LEAF ATTACHMENT	FRUIT
Round	Bell	Simple	Alternate	Berry

BOG ROSEMARY
Andromeda glaucophylla

Family: Heath (Ericaceae)

Height: 1-2' (30-60 cm); shrub

Flower: a small cluster of 1-4 bell-shaped, white-to-pink flowers, ¼-½" (.6-1 cm) long, sits at the end of an arching woody stem; 5 petals fuse together to form an urn-shaped flower with a very narrow opening

Leaf: narrow, toothless, evergreen leaves 1-2" (2.5-5 cm) long, alternate along the woody stem; each leaf has conspicuous white hairs underneath when young; turns a light brown with age

Fruit: round, pink, pod-like container that dries to brown

Bloom: spring, summer

Cycle/Origin: perennial, native

Habitat: wet, acid bogs and muskegs, usually within a conifer woods

Range: northern and eastern two-thirds of the state, especially in the Arrowhead Region and BWCA

Stan's Notes: A common woody shrub of the Canoe Country, the Bog Rosemary can often be seen along the edges of streams and occasionally in dryer places. Its evergreen leaves have an inward-rolled leaf edge (margin). The species name, *glaucophylla*, is Latin for "white leaf," referring to the dense white hairs covering the underside of each leaf. Similar to Labrador Tea (pg. 281).

FLOWER TYPE	LEAF TYPE	LEAF ATTACHMENT	FRUIT
Bell	Simple	Alternate	Pod

fruit

WINTERGREEN
Gaultheria procumbens

Family: Heath (Ericaceae); shrub

Height: 2-6" (5-15 cm)

Flower: nodding, white (sometimes pink) bell-shaped flowers, ⅓" (.8 cm) long, consisting of 5 fused petals; 1-3 flowers per plant

Leaf: smooth (but leathery), round fine-toothed, evergreen leaves, 1-2" (2.5-5 cm) wide, often dark, shiny, waxy

Fruit: bright red pulpy berry with a strong wintergreen taste

Bloom: spring, summer

Cycle/Origin: perennial, native

Habitat: dry, shade, conifer woods

Range: northeastern half of the state, especially in the BWCA

Stan's Notes: Also called Teaberry or Checkerberry, Wintergreen is a low, creeping, evergreen shrub with leathery leaves. Every part of the plant is strongly aromatic and has been used to flavor teas, candies and medicines. The plant contains methyl salicylate, an oil closely related to aspirin that has a similar effect. Its red berries are edible. The current year's leaves are bright green while those of previous years are brownish green. Leaves stay on the plant and remain green under the snow. Fruit is eaten by birds and wildlife. Often associated with white pines, preferring an acidic, well-drained soil.

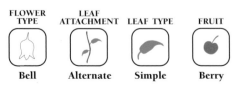

FLOWER TYPE	LEAF ATTACHMENT	LEAF TYPE	FRUIT
Bell	Alternate	Simple	Berry

CUT-LEAVED TOOTHWORT
Cardamine concatenata

Family: Mustard (Brassicaceae)

Height: 8-10" (20-25 cm)

Flower: a small collection of 3-15 regular white or pale lavender flowers, ½" (1 cm) long, each with 4 petals

Leaf: a whorl of 3-lobed leaves; each leaf, 2-5" (5-12.5 cm) wide, has 3 main lobes and many coarse teeth

Fruit: a narrow, upturned pod-like capsule

Bloom: spring

Cycle/Origin: perennial, native

Habitat: shade, deciduous woods

Range: southeastern half of the state

Stan's Notes: One of the spring ephemeral wildflowers (it flowers early, before the leaves of the forest trees sprout and block out sunlight). Cut-leaved Toothwort grows in small patches that dot the floor of deciduous woods. It dies back to the ground by midsummer. Its common name refers to its deeply cut lobes of the leaves, which resemble teeth. The name "wort" means "common," referring to it being a common springtime plant. A host plant for the Checkered White butterfly caterpillar.

FLOWER TYPE	LEAF TYPE	LEAF ATTACHMENT	FRUIT
Regular	Simple Lobed	Whorl	Pod

STAR FLOWER
Trientalis borealis

Family: Primrose (Primulaceae)

Height: 4-8" (10-20 cm)

Flower: usually only 1-2 star-shaped, white flowers, ½" (1 cm) wide, rise on thin delicate stalks above leaves; individual flowers have 7 sharply pointed petals

Leaf: a single whorl of 5-7 lance-shaped leaves, 2-4" (5-10 cm) long, at the top of a delicate stalk

Fruit: a 5-sided pod-like capsule that contains many seeds

Bloom: spring, summer

Cycle/Origin: perennial, native

Habitat: wet, shade, conifer woods, deciduous woods

Range: northern two-thirds of the state, especially in the BWCA

Stan's Notes: The Star Flower is a small, delicate plant that grows in moist areas, often with mosses and usually in clumps or clusters. Its seven petals are unusual in the plant world. Its common name comes from its pointed petals, which form a star. Its genus name, *Trientalis*, comes from the Latin word meaning "one-third of a foot," referring to the height of the plant. The species name, *borealis*, comes from the Latin word meaning "northern," referring to its northern growing range.

FLOWER TYPE	LEAF TYPE	LEAF ATTACHMENT	FRUIT
Regular	Simple	Whorl	Pod

RATTLESNAKE ROOT
Prenanthes alba

Family: Aster (Asteraceae)

Height: 2-5' (60-150 cm)

Flower: small, white-to-cream-colored and purple-tinged bell-shaped flowers, ½" (1 cm) long, hang in clusters of 3-4; individual flowers have 8-15 petals

Leaf: large, coarsely toothed, triangular-shaped leaves, up to 8" (20 cm) long; leaves have multiple sharp lobes and are highly variable, with some leaves lacking lobes

Bloom: summer, fall

Cycle/Origin: perennial, native

Habitat: wet, shade, deciduous woods

Range: throughout

Stan's Notes: Rattlesnake Root's characteristic leaves and purplish green stems help identify this plant of moist woodlands. One of many species of *Prenanthes* found in Minnesota, it is also called White Lettuce. The common name, Rattlesnake Root, comes from its history of use as a snake bite remedy. The sap from its roots and stem was sometimes used to treat dysentery.

FLOWER TYPE

Bell

LEAF TYPE

Simple Lobed

LEAF ATTACHMENT

Alternate

SPRING BEAUTY
Claytonia virginica

Family: Purslane (Portulacaceae)

Height: 6-10" (15-25 cm)

Flower: showy, upright flowers, ½-¾" (1-2 cm) wide, whitish with pink veining; each flower is made up of 5 petals with a slightly yellow-tinted center

Leaf: usually a single pair of oppositely attached grass-like leaves, 2-4" (5-10 cm) long, located about midway up the stem

Bloom: spring

Cycle/Origin: perennial, native

Habitat: wet, shade, deciduous woods, clearings in woods

Range: eastern half of state excluding the Arrowhead Region

Stan's Notes: Spring Beauty often grows in large patches, reproducing from small, underground, potato-like tubers. The flower's pink veins act as signposts or runways to guide insects to the nectar. As they "taxi in," the insects brush against stamens, loading up on pollen, then off to another flower where they drop a few grains on the receptive stigma. This plant's numbers have been reduced because of the over-gathering of these tubers for food, so please don't dig them up. One of many in the Purslane family, a group of about 600 species of plants worldwide, Spring Beauty is a very attractive flower that flowers early in spring, hence its common name. A variety can be purchased at your local garden center to grow in your garden.

FLOWER TYPE	LEAF TYPE	LEAF ATTACHMENT
Regular	**Simple**	**Opposite**

SNOW TRILLIUM
Trillium nivale

Family: Lily (Liliaceae)

Height: 2-6" (5-15 cm)

Flower: a single white flower, ½-1" (1-2.5 cm) wide, stands erect above a whorl of leaves; flower is made up of 3 white petals and 3 green petal-like sepals

Leaf: a single whorl of 3 toothless, stalkless, lance-shaped leaves with rounded tips

Fruit: a single red-to-purple berry

Bloom: spring

Cycle/Origin: perennial, native

Habitat: wet, shade, deciduous woods

Range: southern one-third of the state, mostly in the southeastern corner

Stan's Notes: Also called Dwarf White Trillium, Snow Trillium is one of four species of Trillium in Minnesota. Two of these four species, including Snow Trillium, have a flower that sits above a whorl of leaves (the flower sits below the leaf whorl in the other two species). The Snow Trillium is the smallest and earliest blooming of the Trilliums, often blooming while some snow remains on the ground, hence the common name. They don't grow well in gardens and should be enjoyed in the wild and not dug up.

FLOWER TYPE	LEAF TYPE	LEAF ATTACHMENT	FRUIT

Regular	Simple	Whorl	Berry

single

INDIAN PIPE
Monotropa uniflora

Family: Indian Pipe (Monotropaceae)

Height: 3-9" (7.5-22.5 cm)

Flower: a single, waxy, white (sometimes pink) bell-like flower, ½-1" (1-2.5 cm) long, hangs from the end of each white stem; the hanging bells are formed by 4-5 petals

Leaf: very small scale-like leaves, ¼" (.6 cm) long, often go unnoticed

Fruit: oval pod-like capsule that turns black as seeds mature

Bloom: summer

Cycle/Origin: perennial, native

Habitat: dry, shade, conifer woods, deciduous woods

Range: throughout the eastern half of the state

Stan's Notes: A very unique plant of the forest, Indian Pipe lacks chlorophyll, so it always appears white and turns black with age or if picked. It doesn't make food for itself like other plants, and instead gets its nourishment from dead or decaying plant material through a mutually beneficial fungal relationship called mycorrhiza. Some believe it might be a parasitic plant, living off other living plants, killing its host. It often grows in small clumps but can grow alone. The species name, *uniflora*, means "one flower," describing its one bell flower per plant. The flower turns upright after pollination, describing the genus name, *Monotropa* (one turn).

FLOWER TYPE

Bell

FRUIT

Pod

ARROWHEAD
Sagittaria latifolia

Family: Water-Plantain (Alismataceae)

Height: aquatic

Flower: white flowers, ½-1" (1-2.5 cm) wide, in whorls of 3 sit on an erect stalk; each flower has 3 oval white-to-green petals around the center

Leaf: large, toothless, arrowhead-shaped leaves, 5-16" (12.5-40 cm) long, with strong veins; each leaf is held above the water on its own stalk; stems arise from base of plant

Bloom: summer, fall

Cycle/Origin: perennial, native

Habitat: an aquatic plant of wet areas, found along slow-moving streams, ponds and quiet lakes

Range: throughout

Stan's Notes: Over ten species of Arrowhead are found in the U.S., but only two occur in Minnesota, with this being the most common. The leaves can be extremely narrow or very wide. It grows in the muddy bottoms of calm waters and produces edible tubers eaten by muskrats, swans, geese and ducks, hence its other common name, Duck Potatoes. These tubers, also called wapatoo, have long been gathered by people for food. Leaves are held above the water surface, unlike the floating leaves of the White Water Lily (pg. 301). A favorite food of migrating Tundra Swans and also eaten by Trumpeter Swans.

FLOWER TYPE	LEAF TYPE	LEAF ATTACHMENT
Regular	Simple Lobed	Basal

WHITE LADY'S SLIPPER
Cypripedium candidum

Family: Orchid (Orchidaceae)

Height: 6-12" (15-30 cm)

Flower: each stalk produces 1 small white flower, ½-1" (1-2.5 cm) long; flowers are made up of an inflated lower petal (slipper) with purple streaks, and 3 pointed and twisted greenish brown bracts above

Leaf: basal, heavily parallel-veined lance-shaped leaves, 6-10" (15-25 cm) long

Fruit: pod-like capsule, 1" (2.5 cm) long

Bloom: spring

Cycle/Origin: perennial, native

Habitat: wet, sun, moist prairies, edge of wetlands, along rivers

Range: in a band from the northwestern corner to the southeastern corner of the state, along the Minnesota River Valley

Stan's Notes: Also called Small White Orchid, White Lady's Slipper is found growing in moist prairies and wetlands and along rivers. One of the smallest orchids in Minnesota, it produces only one flower per stem (rarely two). Look for leaves on the flower stalk to help identify this plant. Please enjoy these flowers where you find them and do not pick or attempt to transplant. Most of our native orchids take nearly 20 years to mature and produce their dust-like seeds.

FLOWER TYPE	LEAF TYPE	LEAF ATTACHMENT	LEAF ATTACHMENT	FRUIT
Irregular	**Simple**	**Alternate**	**Basal**	**Pod**

BLACK SNAKEROOT
Sanicula marilandica

Family: Parsley (Apiaceae)

Height: 1-4' (30-120 cm)

Flower: 3-5 round clusters of white-to-cream flowers, each ½-1" (1-2.5 cm) in diameter, sit on the end of thin stalks

Leaf: a large leaf, 3-5" (7.5-12.5 cm) wide, with 3-5 leaflets, each of which has 3 lobes; leaf edges have alternating large and small teeth

Bloom: summer

Cycle/Origin: perennial, native

Habitat: dry woods, along forest edges

Range: throughout

Stan's Notes: A very common plant of forests throughout Minnesota, the Black Snakeroot's small flowers produce small oval seeds covered with tiny hairs and bristles, allowing the seeds to spread by "hitchhiking" in the fur of animals. Like all plants of the Parsley family, it has flat or round clusters of flowers. This wildflower is one of many different plants with the common name "Snakeroot," and one of several very similar species that occur in Minnesota. Its genus name, *Sanicula,* comes from the Latin *sanare,* or "to heal," as it was once thought that this group of plants harbored healing powers.

CLUSTER TYPE	LEAF TYPE	LEAF ATTACHMENT	LEAF ATTACHMENT
Round	Palmate	Alternate	Clasping

FALSE LILY-OF-THE-VALLEY
Maianthemum canadense

Family: Lily (Liliaceae)

Height: 2-6" (5-15 cm)

Flower: small spike cluster of white flowers on a stalk, ½-3" (1-7.5 cm) tall; individual flowers, ⅛" (.5 cm) wide, are star-shaped; 2 petals and 2 petal-like sepals give the appearance of 4 petals

Leaf: 2 (occasionally 3) pointed, lance-shaped leaves alternate along a zigzag stem; stalkless leaves

Fruit: green berries turn dull red with dull white speckles

Bloom: spring

Cycle/Origin: perennial, native

Habitat: shade, conifer woods, deciduous woods

Range: throughout, except for the southwestern corner

Stan's Notes: Also called Wild Lily-of-the-Valley or Canada Mayflower, this low plant of conifer and deciduous forests can be found nearly throughout the state. Its stem is often zigzagged, going back and forth between alternating leaves. It grows in large mats connected by an underground root system (rhizome).

CLUSTER TYPE	FLOWER TYPE	LEAF TYPE	LEAF ATTACHMENT	FRUIT
Spike	Regular	Simple	Alternate	Berry

WHITE CLOVER
Trifolium repens

Family: Pea or Bean (Fabaceae)

Height: 4-10" (10-25 cm)

Flower: white (tinged with pink), fragrant, pea-like, irregular flowers, ¼" (.6 cm) wide, form round cluster, 1" (2.5 cm) wide, on a single long stalk

Leaf: 3 leaflets grow on a long basal stalk to form a compound leaf, 1½" (4 cm) wide; individual leaflets, ¼-½" (.6-1 cm) wide, are round with fine teeth and have a characteristic, dusty white, triangular marking

Bloom: spring, summer, fall

Cycle/Origin: perennial, non-native

Habitat: dry, sun, lawns, fields

Range: throughout

Stan's Notes: Well known for occasionally producing a four-leaf clover, White Clover is a Eurasian import that has found a comfortable home in lawns across North America. It spreads by an aboveground stem that roots at each leaf attachment (node). The genus name, *Trifolium*, describes its three leaflets, while the species name, *repens*, refers to its "creeping" habit of growth. Look for the dusty white triangular markings on its leaves to help you identify this sometimes "lucky" plant. White clover is very attractive to a number of butterfly species including skippers, blues, sulphurs and hairstreaks.

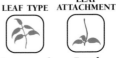

CLUSTER TYPE	FLOWER TYPE	LEAF TYPE	LEAF ATTACHMENT
Round	Irregular	Compound	Basal

fruit

WILD STRAWBERRY
Fragaria virginiana

Family: Rose (Roseaceae)

Size: 3-6" (7.5-15 cm)

Flower: 2-10 white flowers, ¾" (2 cm) wide; each flower has 5 round petals surrounding a yellow center

Leaf: each 3-part basal leaf, 3" (7.5 cm) wide, sits on a long hairy stalk; each leaflet, 1" (2.5 cm) long, is coarsely toothed

Fruit: bright red berry

Bloom: spring

Cycle/Origin: perennial, native

Habitat: dry, sun, edges of woods

Range: throughout

Stan's Notes: Often growing in large patches, Common Strawberry produces some of the sweetest tasting wild berries. This is the original plant from which cultivated strawberries are derived. One of several species of strawberry in Minnesota, it is common just about anywhere in the state. Flowers and fruit are always on stems separate from the leaves.

FLOWER TYPE	LEAF TYPE	LEAF ATTACHMENT	FRUIT
Regular	Compound	Basal	Berry

DUTCHMAN'S BREECHES
Dicentra cucullaria

Family: Fumitory (Fumariaceae)

Height: 4-12" (10-30 cm)

Flower: a collection of waxy flowers, unusually shaped, ¾" (2 cm) long, white-to-pink with yellow tips; each flower is made up of 4 petals and 2 large inflated tubes (spurs) that appear like upside-down pants

Leaf: greenish gray leaves, paler in color beneath and deeply divided, arise from the base of the plant; each leaf has a soft feathery appearance

Fruit: oblong pod-like container that opens at the base

Bloom: spring

Cycle/Origin: perennial, native

Habitat: deciduous woods

Range: throughout

Stan's Notes: A spring ephemeral, Dutchman's Breeches blooms and sets seed each spring before the trees above it have a chance to sprout leaves. Its genus name, *Dicentra*, is derived from the Greek word for "two-spurred," and refers to its long inflated flower spurs that contain the nectar. Only spring bumblebees with a mouth part (proboscis) long enough to delve deep into the flower can sip nectar from its flowers. Some insects have developed a way around this long tube and "cheat" by chewing a hole in the spur to access the nectar.

CLUSTER TYPE	FLOWER TYPE	LEAF TYPE	LEAF ATTACHMENT	FRUIT
Spike	Irregular	Compound	Basal	Pod

CANADA VIOLET
Viola canadensis

Family: Violet (Violaceae)

Height: 8-16" (20-40 cm)

Flower: white, typically violet-shaped flower, ¾-1" (2-2.5 cm) wide, with a yellow center, sits on a slender, purplish stalk; flowers stand above the leaves and are often tinged pink with age

Leaf: thin purplish stalks with sparse hairs hold wide heart-shaped leaves, 1-3" (2.5-7.5 cm) wide, lacking teeth

Bloom: spring, summer

Cycle/Origin: perennial, native

Habitat: wet, cool, shade, rich deciduous woods

Range: throughout

Stan's Notes: One of the few "stalked" violets, the Canada Violet's flowers rise from a stalk rather than the more typical single basal flower stalk arrangement of most violets. It grows in patches from aboveground runners (stolons), and is one of the few violets that emit a fragrance. Once established, Canada Violet grows well as a garden plant. A good plant for a shady part of your yard or garden.

FLOWER TYPE

Irregular

LEAF TYPE

Simple

LEAF ATTACHMENT

Alternate

fruit

BLUEBEAD LILY
Clintonia borealis

Family: Lily (Liliaceae)

Height: 6-10" (15-25 cm)

Flower: 3-6 creamy, yellow-to-white, slightly drooping flowers per stalk, each approximately ¾-1" (2-2.5 cm) long, and made up of 6 petals (3 petals and 3 petal-like sepals)

Leaf: 2-4 simple, lance-shaped, toothless leaves, 5-8" (12.5-20 cm) long; thick and fleshy

Fruit: numerous shiny, blue-to-black oval berries, ½" (1 cm)

Bloom: spring

Cycle/Origin: perennial, native

Habitat: damp woods, mostly conifer

Range: northern and eastern half of the state from the Twin Cities north and east, BWCA

Stan's Notes: Also called Yellow Clintonia due to its yellowish flowers, the Bluebead Lily has poisonous berries, proving that not all blue berries are edible. Its leaves are thick and fleshy, ooze clear fluids when broken, and smell like cucumbers when crushed. Look closely for silky white hairs along the leaves' edges (margins). The name of this very common plant of the Canoe Country honors the late New York governor DeWitt Clinton (1769-1828).

FLOWER TYPE	LEAF TYPE	LEAF ATTACHMENT	FRUIT
	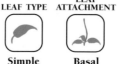		
Regular	Simple	Basal	Berry

INDIAN HEMP
Apocynum cannabinum

Family: Dogbane (Apocynaceae)

Height: 1-3' (30-90 cm)

Flower: a round cluster, 1" (2.5 cm) wide, of 2-10 tiny, whitish green flowers, each ⅓" (.8 cm) wide with 5 petals, found at the end of an erect stalk

Leaf: oval-shaped, toothless leaves, often have a wavy edge (margin)

Fruit: long, thin pod-like capsules, 3-8" (7.5-20 cm), that open along one side, revealing seeds attached to long tufts of white fuzz that help carry them on the wind

Bloom: summer

Cycle/Origin: perennial, native

Habitat: moist, sun, along roads, deciduous woods

Range: throughout, except for the Arrowhead Region

Stan's Notes: Indian Hemp is a tall perennial plant with a single main stem that branches out into many spreading stems. A close relative of the milkweed, it produces a thick, white milky juice in its stem and leaves; this juice contains cardiac glycosides that cause hot flashes, rapid heartbeat and fatigue. Insects avoid this plant because of the poisonous juice. Like Dogbane, its close relative, Indian Hemp's long stems, when dried and peeled, make a strong cord once used by Native Americans, hence its common name. Fibrous stems of old plants are often used by orioles to construct nests.

CLUSTER TYPE	FLOWER TYPE	LEAF TYPE	LEAF ATTACHMENT	FRUIT
		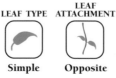		
Round	Regular	Simple	Opposite	Pod

RUE ANEMONE
Thalictrum thalictroides

Family: Buttercup (Ranunculaceae)

Height: 4-8" (10-20 cm)

Flower: 2-3 white-to-pink (or lavender) flowers with a green center made up of 5-10 petal-like sepals, 1" (2.5 cm) wide

Leaf: a whorl of 5-8 lobed leaves grows just below the flowers; each leaf, 1" (2.5 cm) long, has 3 points (teeth) ending with a rounded tip

Bloom: spring

Cycle/Origin: perennial, native

Habitat: wet, deciduous woods

Range: from the Twin Cities south and east

Stan's Notes: A woodland early spring bloomer, Rue Anemone usually grows in large groups, carpeting the forest floor. At about 3-4" (7.5-10 cm) from the ground, its single stem branches into many stems and flower stalks, supporting leaves and a total of two to five flowers, one flower per stalk. Its flower color ranges widely from white to pink to lavender. While its leaves are similar to anemones, this plant is not a true anemone. Its flowers lack nectar, attracting insects instead by the color and shape of the flower. It reproduces mainly by underground roots. Its common name "Rue" comes from the similarity of its leaves to those of the meadow rues (p. 283 and 295).

FLOWER TYPE	LEAF TYPE	LEAF ATTACHMENT
Regular	**Simple Lobed**	**Whorl**

WHITE TROUT LILY
Erythronium albidum

Family: Lily (Liliaceae)

Height: 5-10" (12.5-25 cm)

Flower: each stalk produces a single hanging white flower, 1" (2.5 cm) wide; each flower has a yellow center, sometimes tinted with violet on the back, and 6 backward-curving petals that are actually, 3 petals and 3 petal-like sepals

Leaf: a pair of elliptical, pointed basal leaves, up to 8" (20 cm) long, with brownish purple spots and streaks

Fruit: egg-shaped pod-like container

Bloom: spring

Cycle/Origin: perennial, native

Habitat: dry, deciduous woods

Range: southern two-thirds of the state

Stan's Notes: Also called Dogtooth Violet, White Trout Lily is a member of the Lily family, not a violet. The common name "Trout" comes from its mottled leaves, which resemble the coloring of a Brown Trout. One of the most common spring wildflowers found carpeting deciduous forest floors, the White Trout Lily reproduces mostly by underground bulbs. Nearly identical to the Yellow Trout Lily (pg. 337), except for the color of the flower.

FLOWER TYPE	LEAF TYPE	LEAF ATTACHMENT	FRUIT
Bell	Simple	Basal	Pod

WOOD ANEMONE
Anemone quinquefolia

Family: Buttercup (Ranunculaceae)

Height: 4-8" (10-20 cm)

Flower: a single white flower, 1" (2.5 cm) wide, rises above the leaves; each flower has 5 petal-like white sepals (sepals can be pink or rarely purple)

Leaf: a set of whorled leaves; each individual leaf has 3-5 coarse-toothed and pointed lobes, 1¼" (3 cm) long

Bloom: spring

Cycle/Origin: perennial, native

Habitat: dry, shade, openings and edges of deciduous woods

Range: throughout, except for the southwestern corner

Stan's Notes: Also called Mayflower, Wood Anemone is a common spring wildflower (it flowers before the trees above have a chance to set leaves). While its flowers are usually white, they are sometimes pink. It reproduces along a horizontal underground rootstock (rhizome) to form large mats or patches of growth. The genus name, *Anemone*, comes from the Greek word for "wind," and refers to the plant's thin stalk, which trembles in the wind. Plants that bloom are older than non-bloomers. It may take 5 years or more to reach flowering age.

FLOWER TYPE

Regular

LEAF TYPE

Simple Lobed

LEAF ATTACHMENT

Whorl

WHITE CAMPION
Silene alba

Family: Pink (Caryophyllaceae)

Height: 1-3' (30-90 cm)

Flower: many white flowers, 1" (2.5 cm) wide, each with 5 deeply notched petals, giving the appearance of 10 petals; large, dark-veined, green "bladders" (calyx) behind each flower

Leaf: hairy lance-shaped leaves, 1-4" (2.5-10 cm) long

Bloom: summer

Cycle/Origin: annual, non-native

Habitat: dry, fields, gardens, along roads, disturbed soils

Range: throughout

Stan's Notes: An evening-blooming plant, White Campion's many white flowers are easy to see at night and attract night-flying insects, such as moths. Its male and female flowers are found on separate plants (called dioecious), and its petals retract back into each flower's sticky "bladder" during the day. A European import, it often pops up in untended gardens, and along roads and open fields. Also called Bladder Campion or Evening Lychnis. This plant grows among other plants and its many branches, stems and joints give it a bushy appearance. Seeds shake out of its capsule on the winter winds. Good food for finches and sparrows.

FLOWER TYPE   **LEAF TYPE**   **LEAF ATTACHMENT**

Regular   **Simple**   **Opposite**

HOARY ALYSSUM
Berteroa incana

Family: Mustard (Brassicaceae)

Height: 1-3' (30-90 cm)

Flower: spike cluster, 1" (2.5 cm) tall, of tiny white flowers, ¼" (.6 cm), each consisting of 4 petals; each petal is partly divided (notched) so each flower looks like it is made up of 8 petals

Leaf: thin lance-shaped leaves, ½" (1 cm) long, covered with pale white hairs, giving them a downy appearance; leaves alternate along a single stem that divides near the top

Fruit: many small, round, pointed, pod-like containers, ¼" (.6 cm) long, covered with downy hair

Bloom: summer, fall

Cycle/Origin: annual, non-native

Habitat: dry, sun, open fields, along roads, disturbed sites

Range: throughout

Stan's Notes: The Hoary Alyssum usually appears as a single-stemmed erect plant that branches only near the top to accommodate spike clusters of small white flowers. The entire plant is covered with gray-to-white hair, hence the common name, "Hoary." Its flowers have four petals, indicating a member of the Mustard family. A European import, two species of alyssum grow in North America. A host plant for Cabbage butterfly caterpillars.

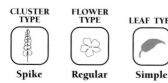

CLUSTER TYPE	FLOWER TYPE	LEAF TYPE	LEAF ATTACHMENT	FRUIT
Spike	Regular	Simple	Alternate	Pod

THIMBLEWEED
Anemone virginiana

Family: Buttercup (Ranunculaceae)

Height: 2-3' (60-90 cm)

Flower: thimble-shaped center of flower, 1" (2.5 cm) tall, is about twice as long as it is wide; 5 white petal-like sepals, ¾" (2 cm) long; each flower is on a single, long, thin stalk

Leaf: basal leaves are divided into 3 coarsely toothed lobes, 3" (7.5 cm) long; leaves on the stem (cauline) are similar but smaller and are whorled around stem

Bloom: summer

Cycle/Origin: perennial, native

Habitat: dry, sun, rocky outcroppings, open woods

Range: throughout

Stan's Notes: Also called the Virginia Thimbleweed. One of a number of species of *Anemone* in Minnesota, the Thimbleweed is a single-stemmed plant with two to three sets of whorled leaves (each group of whorled leaves has two, three or five leaves). The length of the flower's center, or "thimble," differentiates the Thimbleweed from the Long-fruited Thimbleweed (pg. 257). Like some members of the Buttercup family, its flower lacks petals, and instead has large petal-like sepals. Thimble-shaped seed heads turn cottony with many small seeds.

FLOWER TYPE	LEAF TYPE	LEAF ATTACHMENT	LEAF ATTACHMENT

Regular	Simple Lobed	Basal	Whorl

PUSSYTOES
Antennaria neglecta

Family: Aster (Asteraceae)

Height: 4-12" (10-30 cm)

Flower: a 1" (2.5 cm) round cluster of 3-10 white, fuzzy flowers, ¼" (.6 cm) long, on top of a single fuzzy stem

Leaf: spoon-shaped, single-veined basal leaves, 1-2" (2.5-5 cm) long, are covered in white hairs, with a fuzzy appearance; leaves on the stems are very small, ¼" (.6 cm) long, and often go unnoticed

Bloom: spring

Cycle/Origin: perennial, native

Habitat: dry, sun or shade, open woods, rocky outcroppings

Range: throughout

Stan's Notes: Although its flowers are white, its dense covering of hairs make Pussytoes appear to be gray. The bristly flower heads resemble a cat's paw, hence the common name. Other species of Pussytoes are slightly taller and have between three to five veins on the basal leaves as opposed to the single vein of this plant. Often grows to form a dense mat. It can be very difficult to correctly identify this plant. This plant is so variable that even botanists don't agree on the number of species or where the species are found. This is an allelopathic plant, giving off chemicals that "poison" the soil for other plants, reducing competition for moisture and sunlight.

CLUSTER TYPE	FLOWER TYPE	LEAF TYPE	LEAF ATTACHMENT
		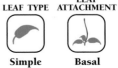	
Round	Composite	Simple	Basal

CANADA ANEMONE
Anemone canadensis

Family: Buttercup (Ranunculaceae)

Height: 1-2' (30-60 cm)

Flower: a regular flower, 1-1½" (2.5-4 cm) wide, with 5 white petal-like sepals and a yellow center; each flower sits on a single, long, hairy stalk

Leaf: long-stalked, coarsely toothed basal leaves are deeply divided into 3 narrow segments; leaves on the stalk (cauline) are coarsely toothed, stalkless, whorled, deeply lobed and usually divided into 3 parts

Bloom: spring, summer

Cycle/Origin: perennial, native

Habitat: wet meadows, prairies

Range: throughout

Stan's Notes: Also called the Canada Windflower or Meadow Anemone, the Canada Anemone is a perennial that spreads by horizontal underground roots (rhizomes), which often cause it to grow in large patches. Its flowers are actually the yellow center, while the white petals are modified leaves (sepals). Over 80 species of anemone can be found throughout the world, about 25 species in North America alone, some of which are grown as garden flowers. All have a whorl of leaves on the stalk (cauline) just below the flower.

FLOWER TYPE

Regular

LEAF TYPE

Simple Lobed

LEAF ATTACHMENT

Basal

LEAF ATTACHMENT

Whorl

NODDING TRILLIUM
Trillium cernuum

Family: Lily (Liliaceae)

Height: 6-24" (15-60 cm)

Flower: a single white flower, 1-1½" (2.5-4 cm) wide, made up of 3 white petals and 3 green sepals; flowers hang below a whorl of leaves on a short stalk, 1-2" (2.5-5 cm) long

Leaf: a single whorl of 3 wavy-edged, toothless and stalkless diamond-shaped leaves with pointed tips

Fruit: a single red-to-purple berry

Bloom: spring, summer

Cycle/Origin: perennial, native

Habitat: wet, shade, deciduous woods

Range: throughout

Stan's Notes: Nodding Trillium is one of four species of Trillium in Minnesota and one of two species whose flower hangs below the whorl of leaves (the flower sits above the leaf whorl in the other two species). The species name, *cernuum*, comes from the Latin word for "drooping" or "nodding," and refers to the flower position. Its leaves are often confused with that of the Jack-in-the-pulpit (pg. 75). If any part of the plant is picked, the leaves may not be able to produce enough starch and sugar to replenish the bulb to bloom the next year. Enjoy in the wild only!

FLOWER TYPE	LEAF TYPE	LEAF ATTACHMENT	FRUIT
Regular	Simple	Whorl	Berry

YELLOW GENTIAN
Gentiana flavida

Family: Gentian (Gentianaceae)

Height: 1-2' (30-60 cm)

Flower: a round cluster of whitish yellow closed tube flowers, 1-1½" (2.5-4 cm) long, each flower is made up
of 5 fused petals that provide no apparent entrance
into the tube flower

Leaf: toothless and lance-shaped leaves, 5" (12.5 cm)
long and 1½" (4 cm) wide, with 3 main veins;
leaves clasp the stem with their edges bent upwards
to form a trough; lower leaves are opposite and
upper leaves, near flower cluster, are whorled

Fruit: a papery pod roughly the same size and shape of
the flowers contains up to 100 tiny brown seeds

Bloom: fall

Cycle/Origin: perennial, native

Habitat: dry, sun, prairies, along railroad beds, old fields

Range: throughout

Stan's Notes: The Yellow Gentian is also called the Closed
Gentian due to its curiously closed flowers, which keep all but the
largest insects, such as Bumblebees, from forcing themselves
through the top. A wonderful perennial of the prairie, this wildflower can also be grown in a garden, but please do not dig it from
the wild. One of at least seven species of gentian in Minnesota.

CLUSTER TYPE	FLOWER TYPE	LEAF TYPE	LEAF ATTACHMENT	LEAF ATTACHMENT	FRUIT
Round	Tube	Simple	Opposite	Whorl	Pod

fruit

BUNCHBERRY
Cornus canadensis

Family: Dogwood (Cornaceae)

Height: 3-8" (7.5-20 cm)

Flower: 4 white, petal-like bracts, 1½" (4 cm) long, surround a group of tiny green flowers, ⅛" (.3 cm) wide, giving the appearance of a single, large, white flower

Leaf: 4-6 toothless, elliptical leaves with pointed ends and deep curving veins, whorling around a central woody stem

Fruit: tight bunch of bright red berries

Bloom: spring

Cycle/Origin: perennial, native

Habitat: conifer forest floor

Range: northeastern half of the state, north from the Twin Cities, especially in the BWCA

Stan's Notes: Underground stems (rhizomes) spread this smallest member of the Dogwood family in large patches on the forest floor. Each leaf vein runs independently to the leaf's edge. Look for tiny scale-like leaves on the stem just below the whorl of main leaves. A common plant of the North Country, the Bunchberry is related to the Red-twigged Dogwood, a common ornamental shrub. A host plant for Spring Azure butterfly caterpillars.

FLOWER TYPE	LEAF TYPE	LEAF ATTACHMENT	FRUIT
Regular	Simple	Whorl	Berry

BLOODROOT
Sanguinaria canadensis

Family: Poppy (Papaveraceae)

Height: 5-10" (12.5-25 cm)

Flower: large, single, white (sometimes pink) flowers, 1½" (4 cm) wide, each with 8-10 petals and a golden yellow center; each flower on its own pinkish stalk

Leaf: large, bluish green, round leaves, 4-7" (10-18 cm) wide, 5-9 lobes per leaf, sit on a long leafstalk; leaves wrap around flower stalk, opening horizontally (flat) after bloom

Fruit: pod-like capsule splits to reveal many brown seeds

Bloom: spring

Cycle/Origin: perennial, native

Habitat: deciduous woods

Range: throughout

Stan's Notes: These flowers lack nectar, quickly dropping petals after pollination, leaving a large, pointed pod-like capsule. One of the earliest plants, it emerges from nearly frozen soil, flowering well before trees leaf out. Its flowers open on sunny days, closing tightly at night. Leaves unroll in full sun, curling up around the flower stalk at night and on cloudy days. The genus name, *Sanguinaria*, comes from Latin word for "bleeding," describing the red orange juice in the stems and roots, used by many cultures as a dye and insect repellent. Easy to grow in gardens; don't dig it from the wild.

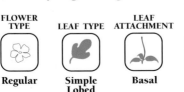

FLOWER TYPE	LEAF TYPE	LEAF ATTACHMENT	FRUIT
Regular	Simple Lobed	Basal	Pod

fruit

BUR CUCUMBER
Sicyos angulatus

Family: Gourd (Cucurbitaceae)

Height: 2-10' (60-300 cm); climbing vine

Flower: a round cluster, 1-2" (2.5-5 cm) wide, of small white flowers, ½" (1 cm) wide, each with 5 pointed petals; the flowering stalk arises from a leaf joint (axis)

Leaf: large maple-like leaves, 4-6" (10-15 cm) wide, each with 5 lobes

Fruit: cluster of up to 10 small pod-like containers, ½-1" (1-2.5 cm) round, each covered with tiny rubbery spines; each pod contains a single seed

Bloom: summer, fall

Cycle/Origin: annual, native

Habitat: wet, shade, deciduous woods, along streams, lakes and wetlands

Range: southern half of the state

Stan's Notes: The Bur Cucumber looks very similar to the Wild Cucumber (pg. 303), but grows in dryer areas. The Bur Cucumber has long, curly forked tendrils and a hairy stem, and its leaves, flower stalks and tendrils all arise from the same location on the vine.

CLUSTER TYPE	FLOWER TYPE	LEAF TYPE	LEAF ATTACHMENT	FRUIT

Round	**Regular**	**Simple Lobed**	**Alternate**	**Pod**

TRAILING ARBUTUS
Epigaea repens

Family: Heath (Ericaceae)

Size: 1-4" (2.5-10 cm)

Flower: a tight round cluster, 1-2" (2.5-5 cm) wide, of many white-to-pink flowers; individual flowers, ¼-½" (.6-1 cm) wide, have 5 flaring petals clustered near the ground, often under the leaves

Leaf: oval, olive green, leathery leaves, 1-3" (2.5-7.5 cm) long; alternate along the trailing woody stem; tiny hairs along the leaf edge (margin)

Fruit: brown pod-like container with 5 segments

Bloom: spring

Cycle/Origin: perennial, native

Habitat: dry, sandy soils, conifer woods

Range: northeastern corner of the state, especially in the BWCA

Stan's Notes: A common, trailing (creeping) wildflower with white (rarely pink) and very fragrant flowers. It is one of the first spring wildflowers to bloom in the BWCA. Five petals fuse at their bases to form a short tube. Not as common as it once was, it seems to be a victim of logging and other disturbances.

CLUSTER TYPE	FLOWER TYPE	LEAF TYPE	LEAF ATTACHMENT	FRUIT
Round	**Regular**	**Simple**	**Alternate**	**Pod**

WHORLED MILKWEED
Asclepias verticillata

Family: Milkweed (Asclepiadaceae)

Height: 6-15" (15-37.5 cm)

Flower: tiny white flowers, ⅛" (.3 cm) wide, form a flat cluster, 1-2" (2.5-5 cm) wide; individual flowers have 5 downward-curving petals and 5 upward-pointing petals, referred to as a crown

Leaf: 3-6 whorled, very narrow needle-like leaves, 1-2" (2.5-5 cm) long

Bloom: summer

Cycle/Origin: perennial, native

Habitat: dry, sun, prairies, rocky soils, along roads

Range: throughout

Stan's Notes: Whorled Milkweed usually has one thin stem that branches near the top into several flat-topped flower clusters. Each flower has a slit that allows an insect's legs to slip inside and emerge with a pair of pollen sacs so the insect can unwittingly pollinate another flower. This complicated process means that only a few flowers become pollinated. Whorled Milkweed often grows in patches in nutrient-poor soils, and like many other milkweeds, it has been used in folk medicine. In fact, its genus name, *Asclepias*, is in honor of Aesculapius, the Greek god of medicine. One of the first plants to come back after prairie fires. Visited by solitary bees and ants for nectar.

CLUSTER TYPE	FLOWER TYPE	LEAF TYPE	LEAF ATTACHMENT
Flat	Irregular	Simple	Whorl

WHITE SNAKEROOT
Ageratina altissima

Family: Aster (Asteraceae)

Height: 1-3' (30-90 cm)

Flower: many tiny, white flowers, ⅛" (.4 cm) wide, form several flat clusters, 1-2" (2.5-5 cm) wide

Leaf: dark green leaves, 2-6" (5-15 cm) long, widest at leaf base with a pointed end and ragged teeth

Bloom: fall

Cycle/Origin: perennial, native

Habitat: dry, shade, edges of deciduous woods

Range: southern half of the state

Stan's Notes: Well known as a fall-blooming wildflower, White Snakeroot grows along the shady edges of deciduous woods. It contains a toxin that can be passed from grazing livestock to humans, causing milk sickness. The often-fatal sickness killed thousands of settlers in the Midwest during the early 19th century, including Abraham Lincoln's mother, Nancy Hanks Lincoln. Today, because of better food availability for cows and modern processing, this is no longer a health concern. Many plants share "Snake" in the common name because of the belief that plants growing in the shade harbor snakes or that the plant might be used for treatment of snakebite. Like other members of the Aster family, the White Snakeroot has composite flowers composed entirely of disk flowers, lacking ray flowers.

CLUSTER TYPE	FLOWER TYPE	LEAF TYPE	LEAF ATTACHMENT
		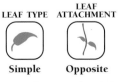	
Flat	Composite	Simple	Opposite

PENNYCRESS
Thlaspi arvense

Family: Mustard (Brassicaceae)

Height: 5-18" (12.5-45 cm)

Flower: small white flowers, ¼" (.6 cm) wide, that grow in short spike clusters, 1-2" (2.5-5 cm) long; individual flowers have 4 petals that form a cross shape

Leaf: stalkless, coarsely toothed, lance-shaped leaves, 2-4" (5-10 cm) long

Fruit: flat, round, notched pod-like containers that look like paper pennies

Bloom: spring

Cycle/Origin: annual, non-native

Habitat: dry, sun, disturbed soils, along roads

Range: throughout

Stan's Notes: The Pennycress is a common annual of disturbed soils, and is often found in farmyards and schoolyards and along trails and roads. Its flowers bloom from the bottom up, and each flower produces a characteristic flat "penny" pod with a large notch on the top. Like all members of the Mustard family, its four flower petals form a cross shape, which helps to identify the plant. Its seedpods turn brown and papery, and its black seeds are hot and peppery and have been used as a pepper substitute. This native of Europe is also called Field Pennycress.

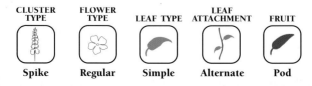

CLUSTER TYPE	FLOWER TYPE	LEAF TYPE	LEAF ATTACHMENT	FRUIT
Spike	Regular	Simple	Alternate	Pod

PEARLY EVERLASTING
Anaphalis margaritacea

Family: Aster (Asteraceae)

Height: 1-3' (30-90 cm)

Flower: a round cluster, 1-2" (2.5-5 cm) wide, made of many individual, white flower heads; individual flowers, ¼" (.6 cm) tall, are composed of white, petal-like bracts surrounding a yellow center (disk flowers)

Leaf: long, narrow, greenish-white leaves, 3-5" (7.5-12.5 cm), alternate along the stem; leaves are densely hairy underneath, causing them to look woolly white

Bloom: summer, fall

Cycle/Origin: perennial, native

Habitat: dry, sun, pastures, along roads, fields

Range: northeastern half of the state, BWCA

Stan's Notes: A common plant of the North Shore of Lake Superior, the Pearly Everlasting blooms from summer to fall. Its stems are covered with soft cottony hairs, and its flower clusters are often dried and used in floral arrangements. While it's the only species of its genus found in North America, individual plants can be highly variable. A host plant for American Painted Lady butterfly caterpillars, one of our over-wintering adult butterflies.

CLUSTER TYPE	FLOWER TYPE	LEAF TYPE	LEAF ATTACHMENT
Round	Composite	Simple	Alternate

FIELD BINDWEED
Convolvulus arvensis

Family: Morning Glory (Convolvulaceae)

Height: 1-6' (30-180 cm); climbing vine

Flower: white, tube or funnel-shaped flowers, 1-2" (2.5-5 cm) wide; 5 petals fuse together to form the flower

Leaf: small, triangular or arrowhead-shaped, toothless leaves, 1-2" (2.5-5 cm) long, alternate along the climbing, twisting stem

Bloom: summer, fall

Growth: perennial, non-native

Habitat: dry, sunny fields, usually creeping along the ground but occasionally climbing on fences or shrubs

Range: throughout the lower two-thirds of the state

Stan's Notes: Very similar to Hedge Bindweed (pg. 275), this wildflower of summer is usually so small that it goes unnoticed until its pure white flowers open on sunny days. Closely related to the Common Blue Morning Glory of the garden, the Field Bindweed seems to prefer disturbed soils, old fields, abandoned lots in cities, and suburban lawns. It grows in large tangled mats, and its flowers are sometimes slightly pink. The genus name, *Convolvulus*, is from the Latin *convolvere*, "to entwine," which accurately describes its growing habit. Lacking tendrils to grasp other plants, it twists its stems around host plants for support, seeking sunlight, a habit that provides its other common name, Possession Vine.

FLOWER TYPE	LEAF TYPE	LEAF ATTACHMENT
Tube	Simple	Alternate

OX-EYE DAISY
Leucanthemum vulgare

Family: Aster (Asteraceae)

Height: 1-3' (30-90 cm)

Flower: a common white-and-yellow flower head, 1-2" (2.5-5 cm) wide, with up to 20 white petals (ray flowers) surrounding a yellow center of disk flowers

Leaf: dandelion-like, lobed, thick, dark green, clasping basal leaves, up to 6" (15 cm) long; stem leaves, 1-2" (2.5-5 cm) long, similar to basal leaves, only smaller

Bloom: spring, summer

Cycle/Origin: perennial, non-native

Habitat: wet or dry, sun, fields, along roads, pastures

Range: throughout, mostly in the northeastern corner

Stan's Notes: Also called the Common Daisy, the Ox-eye Daisy is a European import often seen growing in patches along roads. In poor soil it grows short and erect; in rich soils it grows tall, and its weak stem causes it to fall over and spread out across the ground. Ox-eye Daisy contains pyrethrum, a chemical that repels insects and is used in organic pesticides. This nice garden plant is often overlooked. A very interesting composite of many flowers appearing as one large flower. Each white petal is a separate flower, while the center yellow portion is many individual disk flowers.

FLOWER TYPE	LEAF TYPE	LEAF ATTACHMENT	LEAF ATTACHMENT	LEAF ATTACHMENT
Composite	**Simple Lobed**	**Alternate**	**Basal**	**Clasping**

LONG-FRUITED THIMBLEWEED
Anemone cylindrica

Family: Buttercup (Ranunculaceae)

Height: 2-3' (60-90 cm)

Flower: a long, thimble-shaped flower, 1¼-2" (3-5 cm) tall, with 5 white petal-like sepals, ¾" (2 cm) long; the center "thimble" is about three times as long as it is wide

Leaf: basal leaves are in a whorl of 3; each leaf, 3" (7.5 cm) long, is divided into 3-5 coarsely toothed lobes; leaves on the stem (cauline) look similar to basal leaves, only smaller

Bloom: summer

Cycle/Origin: perennial, native

Habitat: dry, sun, dry prairies

Range: throughout

Stan's Notes: Also called Thimbleweed, one of seven species of *Anemone* in Minnesota. A single-stemmed hairy plant with two to ten sets of whorled leaves (each group of whorled leaves has two, three or five leaves). Several long flower stalks rise above the last set of leaves. The length of the flower center, or "thimble," differentiates the Long-fruited Thimbleweed from the Thimbleweed (pg. 227). Like some members of the Buttercup family, its flower lacks petals, and instead has large petal-like sepals. After pollination, the thimble-shaped seed heads turn cottony with many small seeds.

FLOWER TYPE	LEAF TYPE	LEAF ATTACHMENT	LEAF ATTACHMENT

Regular	**Lobed**	**Basal**	**Whorl**

flower

GARLIC MUSTARD
Alliaria petiolata

Family: Mustard (Brassicaceae)

Height: 1-3' (30-90 cm)

Flower: a round cluster, 1-3" (2.5-7.5 cm) wide, of small white flowers; individual flowers, ¼" (.6 cm) wide, have 4 white petals

Leaf: heart-shaped lower leaves, 3-4" (7.5-10 cm) long, with sharp irregular teeth; smaller, triangular upper leaves, 1-2" (2.5-5 cm) long; all leaves smell strongly of garlic

Fruit: thin pod-like containers, up to 2" (5 cm) long

Bloom: spring, summer

Cycle/Origin: biennial, non-native

Habitat: wet, shade, deciduous woods

Range: throughout

Stan's Notes: A non-native plant of shady woodland borders and roadsides, Garlic Mustard was introduced from Europe. It was once commonly grown in gardens, where its flavorful leaves were cultivated for salads. Its leaves, stems and seedpods have a strong taste of garlic, and its tiny black seeds can be used as a pepper substitute. The four petals, arranged in a cross pattern, unmistakably identify Garlic Mustard as a member of the Mustard family. Seed pods split in half lengthwise to release many tiny black seeds.

CLUSTER TYPE
Round

FLOWER TYPE
Regular

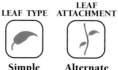

LEAF TYPE
Simple

LEAF ATTACHMENT
Alternate

FRUIT
Pod

259

WHITE PRAIRIE CLOVER
Dalea candida

Family: Pea or Bean (Fabaceae)

Height: 1-2' (30-60 cm)

Flower: very tiny white flowers, ⅙" (.5 cm) long, made up of 5 petals, cluster to form a thick cylindrical-shaped flower head, 1-3" (2.5-7.5 cm) tall

Leaf: powdery green leaves, 1½" (4 cm) long, alternately arranged along the stem; each leaf has 5-9 narrow leaflets, 1½" (4 cm) long

Bloom: summer, fall

Cycle/Origin: perennial, native

Habitat: dry, sun, prairies, along old railroad beds

Range: throughout

Stan's Notes: A delicate plant, White Prairie Clover usually grows singularly, unlike Purple Prairie Clover (pg. 137), which grows in large clumps. Its tiny white flowers bloom from the bottom up on a cone-like head, sometimes resulting in a narrow wreath-like ring of white flowers around the green cylindrical head. This member of the Pea or Bean family lacks the typical pea flower, and has the ability to fix nitrogen into the soil, thus enhancing soil fertility. Like many prairie plants, White Prairie Clover can send roots 5' (1.5 m) into the prairie soil in search of water.

CLUSTER TYPE	LEAF TYPE	LEAF ATTACHMENT
Spike	Compound	Alternate

fruit

RED BANEBERRY
Actaea rubra

Family: Buttercup (Ranunculaceae)

Height: 8-24" (20-60 cm)

Flower: a dense, tight, round cluster, 1-3" (2.5-7.5 cm) wide, of tiny white flowers, each ¼" (.6 cm) wide

Leaf: each leaf has about 5-20 coarse-toothed, oval-shaped, 2" (5 cm) long, leaflets with pointed ends

Fruit: cluster of shiny red berries on a thin green stalk

Bloom: spring

Cycle/Origin: perennial, native

Habitat: wet, shade, deciduous woods

Range: throughout

Stan's Notes: A common perennial of moist deciduous woods, Red Baneberry's leaves and flowers sit in a compact ball at the top of the plant, giving it a bushy appearance. When its flowers open, the petals fall off, leaving just the white stamens. Flowers produce a cluster of shiny, deep red poisonous berries, each rising from its own thin stalk. While they probably won't cause death, its poisonous berries will cause illness if eaten. Nearly identical to White Baneberry (pg. 265), except for the berry color.

CLUSTER TYPE	LEAF TYPE	LEAF ATTACHMENT	FRUIT

Round	Twice Compound	Alternate	Berry

fruit

WHITE BANEBERRY
Actaea pachypoda

Family: Buttercup (Ranunculaceae)

Height: 1-2' (30-60 cm)

Flower: a dense, tight, slightly elongated cluster, 1-3" (2.5-7.5 cm), of tiny white flowers, each ¼" (.6 cm) wide

Leaf: each leaf has about 5-20 coarse-toothed, oval-shaped 2" (5 cm) long, leaflets with pointed ends

Fruit: cluster of shiny white berries, each with a single black spot, grow on a fleshy, reddened stalk

Bloom: spring

Cycle/Origin: perennial, native

Habitat: wet, shade, deciduous woods

Range: throughout

Stan's Notes: A common perennial of moist deciduous woods, White Baneberry's leaves and flowers sit in a compact ball at the top of the plant, giving it a bushy appearance. When its flowers open, the petals fall off, leaving just the white stamens. Flowers produce a cluster of shiny, white poisonous berries, each rising from its own thin stalk. The common name Bane means "to cause death." While they probably won't cause death, its poisonous berries will cause illness if eaten. Nearly identical to Red Baneberry (pg. 263), except for the berry color. The white berries marked with a single black dot look like the eyes of an old china doll, providing its other common name, Doll's Eyes.

CLUSTER TYPE	LEAF TYPE	LEAF ATTACHMENT	FRUIT
Round	Twice Compound	Alternate	Berry

NORTHERN BEDSTRAW
Galium boreale

Family: Madder (Rubiaceae)

Height: 10-36" (25-90 cm)

Flower: dense clusters, 1-3" (2.5-7.5 cm) wide, of tiny white flowers sit at the top of the stalk; each flower, ¼" (.6 cm) wide, has 4 petals that fuse together into a tube at the base

Leaf: a whorl of 4 very narrow, ¼" (.6 cm) wide, linear leaves, ¾-2" (2-5 cm) long, with a pointed end

Bloom: summer

Cycle/Origin: perennial, native

Habitat: dry, sun, prairies, fields, along roads

Range: throughout

Stan's Notes: Also called Snow Bedstraw because of its dense cluster of snow-white flowers, Northern Bedstraw often grows in large clumps and is an impressive sight when in bloom. A square-stemmed plant with a smooth stem and leaves, it is unlike many of the other bedstraws, which have sticky stems. Eleven species of Bedstraw are found in Minnesota, a few of which have a pleasant fragrance when crushed. This plant was once used to stuff mattresses, hence the common name. A member of the same family as coffee, its roasted seeds brew a nice coffee substitute.

CLUSTER TYPE	FLOWER TYPE	LEAF TYPE	LEAF ATTACHMENT
			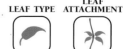
Spike	Regular	Simple	Whorl

COMMON VALERIAN
Valeriana officinalis

Family: Valerian (Valerianaceae)

Height: 2-3' (60-90 cm)

Flower: a compact round cluster, 1-3" (2.5-7.5 cm) wide, of flowers grows at the top of a single stem; individual flowers, white to light pink, ¼" (.6 cm) wide, are made up of 5 petals

Leaf: opposite pairs of deeply divided, fern-like leaves, 1-3" (2.5-7.5 cm) long; each leaf has many (11-21) narrow segments

Bloom: spring, summer

Cycle/Origin: perennial, non-native

Habitat: wet or dry, sun, along roads, old gardens, fields

Range: isolated in and around major cities; common in Duluth and the Twin Cities

Stan's Notes: A native of Eurasia, Common Valerian was originally planted in gardens, but has escaped and is now naturalized in and around Minnesota's major cities. This plant has been used medicinally for many centuries. Its roots contain valeric acid, a chemical that attracts domestic house cats. Also called Garden Heliotrope.

CLUSTER TYPE

Round

FLOWER TYPE

Regular

LEAF TYPE

Lobed

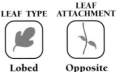

LEAF ATTACHMENT

Opposite

WILD CALLA
Calla palustris

Family: Arum (Araceae)

Height: aquatic

Flower: a large white petal (spathe), 2" (5 cm) long, wraps around a 1" (2.5 cm) tall, club-like cluster (spadix) of tiny yellow flowers, ¼" (.6 cm) wide; the flower is held up to 6" (15 cm) above the water

Leaf: dark green, glossy, heart-shaped leaves, 6" (15 cm) long, on long stalks held above the water surface; leaves are deeply notched where the stalk attaches

Fruit: a tight cluster of bright red berries

Bloom: spring

Cycle/Origin: perennial, native

Habitat: wetlands, ponds, lakes, bogs

Range: throughout

Stan's Notes: Also called Water Arum or Wild Calla Lily, Wild Calla is found in bogs and swamps. All parts of the plant contain oxalic acid, which causes an intense burning sensation if eaten. This plant is characterized by a very interesting two-part flower structure of a club-like spadix wrapped in a flat spathe. The flowers are actually very small and tightly packed at the base of the club-like spadix, (very hard to see). It is closely related to Jack-in-the-pulpit (pg. 75).

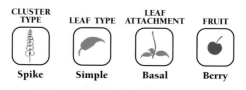

CLUSTER TYPE	LEAF TYPE	LEAF ATTACHMENT	FRUIT
Spike	Simple	Basal	Berry

SHOWY LADY'S SLIPPER
Cypripedium reginae

Family: Orchid (Orchidaceae)

Height: 1-3' (30-90 cm)

Flower: a spectacular flower, 2-3" (5-7.5 cm) tall, with 3 white, pointed, upper petal-like sepals and 1 large, inflated pink-and-white lower petal; the lower inflated petal is often veined in deep pink; hairy, flowering stalks

Leaf: basal leaves, 10" (25 cm) long and up to 2" (5 cm) wide, with deeply ribbed parallel veins, clasp the stem; leaves on flower stem are smaller, clasping, alternating

Fruit: elliptically shaped pod-like capsule, 2" (5 cm) long, containing extremely small seeds

Bloom: summer

Cycle/Origin: perennial, native

Habitat: wet, sun, swamps, moist woods, slow-moving streams

Range: throughout, except for the southwestern corner

Stan's Notes: The official state flower of Minnesota, the Showy Lady's Slipper is the largest and most impressive of the orchids found in the state. It should never be handled or dug up, as this long-lived plant takes up to 15 years to mature and form flowers. Some people get a Poison-Ivy-like rash from touching its stem's glandular hairs. Also called the Pink-and-White Lady's Slipper.

FLOWER TYPE	LEAF TYPE	LEAF ATTACHMENT	LEAF ATTACHMENT	FRUIT
Irregular	**Simple**	**Alternate**	**Basal**	**Pod**

HEDGE BINDWEED
Calystegia sepium

Family: Morning Glory (Convolvulaceae)

Height: 3-10' (90-300 cm); climbing vine

Flower: white-to-pink, tube or funnel-shaped flowers, 2-3" (5-7.5 cm) long; 5 petals fuse together to form the tube flower

Leaf: arrowhead-shaped, toothless leaves, 2-4" (5-10 cm) long, alternate along a vine stem; the base of each leaf extends below its stalk attachment, giving the appearance of ears (basal lobes)

Fruit: papery pod-like container with 4 brown seeds

Bloom: summer, fall

Growth: perennial, native

Habitat: dry, sunny fields, along woodlands

Range: throughout

Stan's Notes: A climbing vine up to 10' (3 m) long, the Hedge Bindweed is often seen on old fences, open fields and climbing on shrubs. Its flowers are highly variable in color, ranging from pure white to pink. They open in the morning and close in the afternoon. Hedge Bindweed flowers will stay open all day if temperatures are cool, but will not open at all if too cold and they usually only last one day. It is closely related to the Common Blue Garden Morning Glory and thirteen other species in North America; similar, but much larger than Field Bindweed (pg. 253).

FLOWER TYPE	LEAF TYPE	LEAF ATTACHMENT	FRUIT
Tube	Simple	Alternate	Pod

BONESET
Eupatorium perfoliatum

Family: Aster (Asteraceae)

Height: 2-4' (60-120 cm)

Flower: numerous, flat, white flowers, each ¼" (.6 cm) in diameter, in a large, flat-topped cluster, 2-3" (5-7.5 cm) wide; multiple tiny flowers give the appearance of a fuzzy cluster

Leaf: large, wrinkly, opposing leaves, 4-8" (10-20 cm) long, join at the base around the stem so that the stem appears to grow through the leaves (perfoliate)

Bloom: summer, fall

Cycle/Origin: perennial, native

Habitat: wet ditches, along roads, prairies, wet meadows

Range: throughout

Stan's Notes: A common, tall, roadside plant, Boneset is easy to identify by its large crinkled leaves and large leaf base that joins around the stem, making the plant appear to be growing through one large leaf (perfoliate). To some healers, this odd leaf growth meant that the plant was useful for setting bones, hence its common name. Boneset Tea, made from the plant's leaves, is said to treat colds and coughs and break fevers. Its stem and leaves are covered in fine whitish hairs. Closely related to Joe-pye Weed (pg. 119) and White Snakeroot (pg. 247), the Boneset is one of the few late-summer-blooming plants. A great nectar plant for Bronze Copper, Monarch, Crescent and Fritillary butterflies.

CLUSTER TYPE	FLOWER TYPE	LEAF TYPE	LEAF ATTACHMENT
		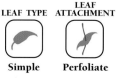	
Flat	**Composite**	**Simple**	**Perfoliate**

TURTLEHEAD
Chelone glabra

Family: Snapdragon (Scrophulariaceae)

Height: 1-3' (30-90 cm)

Flower: tight spike cluster, 2-3" (5-7.5 cm) tall, of many white (sometimes lavender) flowers, 1-1½" (2.5-4 cm) long; 2 petals fuse together to form a tube flower

Leaf: narrow, opposite, lance-shaped leaves, ½-1" (1-2.5 cm) wide and 3-6" (7.5-15 cm) long, with sharp teeth

Bloom: summer, fall

Cycle/Origin: perennial, native

Habitat: wet, sun, moist fields, along streams, wetlands

Range: eastern half of the state

Stan's Notes: Found growing along streams and wetlands, Turtlehead often grows as a single stem topped with a cluster of large white flowers. The shape of the flower resembles the head of a turtle; hence the common name (the genus name, *Chelone*, is Greek for "tortoise"). Look for the narrow, sharp-toothed opposite leaves to help identify this wildflower. A host plant for the very rare Baltimore butterfly. Due to loss of habitat, the Turtlehead is not as common as it once was.

CLUSTER TYPE	FLOWER TYPE	LEAF TYPE	LEAF ATTACHMENT
		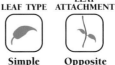	
Spike	Tube	Simple	Opposite

LABRADOR TEA
Ledum groenlandicum

Family: Heath (Ericaceae)

Height: 1-4' (30-120 cm), shrub

Flower: a collection of small white flowers, ⅓-½" (.8-1 cm) wide, form tight round clusters, 2-3" (5-7.5 cm) wide; individual flowers have 5 petals

Leaf: dark green, lance-shaped, evergreen leaves with an inward curled edge (margin) and dense, woolly, orange-brown hairs underneath; leaves are concentrated near the top of its woolly stem

Fruit: pod-like capsule with 5 openings to release seeds

Bloom: spring, summer

Cycle/Origin: perennial, native

Habitat: wet, shade, conifer woods, peat bogs, cedar swamps

Range: northern and eastern half of the state, especially in the BWCA

Stan's Notes: Also known as Hudson's Bay Tea, Labrador Tea is a very common low shrub of the northern bogs. Its leaves contain an aromatic resin that makes a pleasant-tasting tea, and the unique woolly brown hair beneath its leaves makes it one of the easiest plants to identify. Labrador Tea's evergreen leaves remain on the plant year-round.

CLUSTER TYPE	FLOWER TYPE	LEAF TYPE	LEAF ATTACHMENT	FRUIT
Round	Regular	Simple	Alternate	Pod

EARLY MEADOW RUE
Thalictrum dioicum

Family: Buttercup (Ranunculaceae)

Height: 1-3' (30-90 cm)

Flower: a loose, open, round cluster, 2-3" (5-7.5 cm) wide, of whitish green hanging flowers; individual flowers, ¼" (.6 cm) wide, are made up of 4-5 petal-like sepals with showy, thread-like, yellow hanging flower parts (stamens)

Leaf: bluish green leaves that characteristically droop; each leaflet, ½" (1 cm) long, has 3 tooth-like lobes

Fruit: a single ribbed, egg-shaped, pod-like container, ⅛" (.3 cm) long

Bloom: spring

Cycle/Origin: perennial, native

Habitat: wet, shade, moist woods

Range: throughout

Stan's Notes: Sometimes a very difficult species to identify correctly, Early Meadow Rue is a shorter version of the Tall Meadow Rue (pg. 295). It grows in moist or wet depressions within woodlands, and has dark red-to-purple stems and droopy leaves. Male and female flowers grow on different plants, hence the species name, *dioicum*, which is Greek for "two houses" or "two plants." Its flowers are wind pollinated, but are also visited by bees, butterflies and other insects. Often associated with Sugar Maple and Basswood trees.

CLUSTER TYPE

Round

FLOWER TYPE

Bell

LEAF TYPE

Twice Compound

LEAF ATTACHMENT

Alternate

FRUIT

Pod

CATNIP
Nepeta cataria

Family: Mint (Lamiaceae)

Height: 1-3' (30-90 cm)

Flower: a tight spike cluster, 2-4" (5-10 cm) long, of white tube-like flowers, ½" (1 cm) long, made up of 2 large petals; each flower has purplish spots and can range in color from white to lavender

Leaf: opposite, coarsely toothed, arrowhead-shaped leaves, 1-3" (2.5-7.5 cm) long, covered with soft, white, downy hairs; very aromatic when crushed

Bloom: summer, fall

Cycle/Origin: perennial, non-native

Habitat: dry, sun or shade, fields, gardens, along roads, near buildings

Range: throughout

Stan's Notes: A non-native plant thought to come from Asia but probably introduced from Europe as a garden herb, Catnip has been used as a medicinal tea. It contains a terpene-like chemical, nepeta lactone, which works to repel insects. This chemical also attracts cats, from lions to cougars to house cats. Its skunk-like odor and soft downy white hairs help identify this plant, while its square stem and opposite leaves distinguish it as a member of the Mint family.

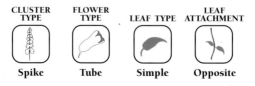

CLUSTER TYPE	FLOWER TYPE	LEAF TYPE	LEAF ATTACHMENT
Spike	Tube	Simple	Opposite

COMMON YARROW
Achillea millefolium

Family: Aster (Asteraceae)

Height: 1-3' (30-90 cm)

Flower: tight, flat-topped, white (sometimes pink) flower clusters, 2-4" (5-10 cm) wide, made up of tiny flower heads, ¼" (.6 cm) wide, each with 4-6 (usually 5) petals

Leaf: narrow, finely divided, fern-like, feathery leaves about 6" (15 cm) long, have a strong aroma and become progressively smaller toward the top; those at the plant's base are stalked, while the upper leaves are not

Bloom: summer, fall

Cycle/Origin: perennial, native

Habitat: dry, sun, deciduous woods, fields, prairies

Range: throughout

Stan's Notes: A common wildflower of open fields and along roads, this is one of three species of *Achillea* found in Minnesota. A native of Eurasia as well as North America, it is uncertain which of our plants were introduced or are native. Often confused with a type of fern because of its leaves, this wildflower grows in large clusters due to a horizontal underground stem (rhizome). The genus name, *Achillea*, comes from the legend that Achilles used the plant to treat bleeding wounds during the Trojan War. The species name, *millefolium*, means "thousand leaves," and refers to each leaf's many divisions, making one leaf look like many. Many cultures have used it as a medicinal herb.

CLUSTER TYPE	FLOWER TYPE	LEAF TYPE	LEAF ATTACHMENT
	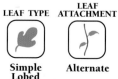	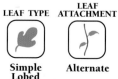	
Flat	Composite	Simple Lobed	Alternate

LARGE-FLOWERED TRILLIUM
Trillium grandiflorum

Family: Lily (Liliaceae)

Height: 8-18" (20-45 cm)

Flower: a single white flower, 2-4" (5-10 cm) wide, grows from a single stalk; 3 white, triangle-shaped, wavy-edged petals are set against 3 pointed, green, petal-like sepals, which look like green petals

Leaf: 3 large, pointed, toothless broad leaves, 3-6" (7.5-15 cm) long, with veins that extend to the leaf's edge

Fruit: a single red berry, 1" (2.5 cm) wide

Bloom: spring

Cycle/Origin: perennial, native

Habitat: rich moist woodlands, deciduous woods

Range: throughout, except for the northeastern and south-western corners

Stan's Notes: Also called White-flowered Trillium, the Large-flowered Trillium is one of four species of trillium found in Minnesota. This species has the largest flower, hence its common and scientific names. It is a protected flower species that should never be picked or dug up (it can be purchased from garden centers, but make sure plants are cultivated from non-wild stock). The Large-flowered Trillium blooms early in spring, occurring alone or in groups, and its white flowers turn pink with age. Seeds are dispersed by ants that carry the seeds back to their underground home and don't eat them.

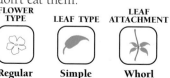

FLOWER TYPE	LEAF TYPE	LEAF ATTACHMENT	FRUIT
Regular	Simple	Whorl	Berry

VIRGIN'S BOWER
Clematis virginiana

Family: Buttercup (Ranunculaceae)

Height: 6-10' (1.8-3 m) climbing vine

Flower: delicate round clusters, 2-4" (5-10 cm) wide, of white flowers, 1" (2.5 cm) wide, with 4 or 5 petal-like sepals with a center of many thin, greenish yellow, hair-like flower parts (stamens and anthers)

Leaf: a 3-part leaf, with each leaflet sharply toothed or lobed, 2" (5 cm) long

Fruit: a group of single seeds, each attached to a single curvy, white, hair-like projection

Bloom: summer

Cycle/Origin: perennial, native

Habitat: shade, along edges of woods

Range: throughout

Stan's Notes: Also called Old Man's Beard, this is one of only two *Clematis* species in Minnesota. The Purple Virgin's Bower grows along the North Shore and features a large blue flower similar to the garden clematis, its close relative. This square-stemmed perennial vine is usually seen growing over fences or shrubs or along riverbanks. Late in summer and fall, the hairy plumes of its pollinated female flowers look like a frosted vine. Seed head has curvy, white hair-like projections, giving the plant the appearance of an old man's beard. This plant can be grown from seed, but should never be dug from the wild.

CLUSTER TYPE	FLOWER TYPE	LEAF TYPE	LEAF ATTACHMENT
		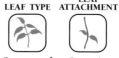	
Round	Regular	Compound	Opposite

WATER HEMLOCK
Cicuta maculata

Family: Carrot (Apiaceae)

Height: 3-6' (90-180 cm)

Flower: delicate flat-topped clusters, 2-4" (5-10 cm) wide, of tiny white flowers, ⅛" (.5 cm) wide

Leaf: lower leaves are larger and sometimes twice compound; upper leaves are compound with individual leaflets, 1" (2.5 cm) long, sharply pointed and toothed, with veins that end at the notches between the teeth

Bloom: summer, fall

Cycle/Origin: perennial, native

Habitat: wet, sun, ditches, along roads, wet meadows

Range: throughout

Stan's Notes: A common plant of wet pastures and along roads and ditches, Water Hemlock is by far the most poisonous plant in Minnesota. A member of the Carrot family, its long taproot smells and tastes like carrot, but just a small amount will lead to convulsions and death. To help correctly identify this dangerous plant, look for the unique network of veins along its toothed leaves: the veins end at the notches between the teeth (as opposed to more common veining of other plants, which run to the tip of the tooth). This plant is closely related to the hemlock that poisoned Socrates.

CLUSTER TYPE	FLOWER TYPE	LEAF TYPE	LEAF ATTACHMENT
		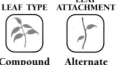	
Flat	Regular	Compound	Alternate

TALL MEADOW RUE
Thalictrum dasycarpum

Family: Buttercup (Ranunculaceae)

Height: 2-8' (60-240 cm)

Flower: round plumy clusters, 3-4" (7.5-10 cm) wide, of dangling whitish green flowers; individual flowers, ⅓" (.8 cm) wide, lack petals and instead have many showy, yellowish, thread-like flower parts (stamens) hanging down

Leaf: bluish green leaves made of up to 25 leaflets; each leaflet, 1" (2.5 cm) long, has 3 tooth-like lobes

Bloom: summer

Cycle/Origin: perennial, native

Habitat: wet, shade, wetlands, along streams

Range: throughout

Stan's Notes: Sometimes a very difficult species to identify correctly, Tall Meadow Rue is a very tall plant with characteristic dark red-to-purple stems and bluish green leaves. Found in wetlands and along streams, it is one of at least four species of *Thalictrum* in Minnesota. Its petals fall off shortly after the flower opens, leaving only the male and female flower parts (stamen and pistils). Its flowers are wind pollinated, but are also visited by bees, butterflies and other insects. Very similar to the shorter Early Meadow Rue (pg. 283).

CLUSTER TYPE	FLOWER TYPE	LEAF TYPE	LEAF ATTACHMENT
Round	Bell	Twice Compound	Alternate

295

QUEEN ANNE'S LACE
Daucus carota

Family: Carrot (Apiaceae)

Height: 1-3' (30-90 cm)

Flower: a flat cluster, 3-5" (7.5-12.5 cm) wide, of tiny white flowers, each ¼" (.6 cm) wide; a single purple-to-black floret sits near the cluster's center, with 3 thin, forked, green bracts beneath the cluster

Leaf: fern-like, with many divisions, up to 8" (20 cm) long

Bloom: summer, fall

Cycle/Origin: biennial, non-native

Habitat: dry, sun, fields, along roads, disturbed soils

Range: southern half of the state

Stan's Notes: Queen Anne's Lace, also called Wild Carrot, is tall with stems covered by tiny hairs. Once a European garden plant, it has escaped to the wild and is considered a weed because of its aggressive growth. Flower clusters dry and curl, forming the bird's nest shape often used in dried flower arrangements. Its long taproot can be dug up, roasted and ground as a coffee substitute. During its first year, the roots are soft enough to eat. It is thought to be the ancestor of the common garden carrot. Take caution: Queen Anne's Lace is sometimes confused with the deadly Water Hemlock (pg. 293). Look closely for Queen Anne's Lace's central purple floret. A host plant for Black Swallowtail butterfly caterpillars.

CLUSTER TYPE	FLOWER TYPE	LEAF TYPE	LEAF ATTACHMENT

Flat	Regular	Twice Compound	Alternate

fruit

FALSE SOLOMON'S SEAL
Maianthemum racemosa

Family: Lily (Liliaceae)

Height: 1-3' (30-90 cm)

Flower: tiny, star-shaped, white flowers, ⅛" (.3 cm) wide, grow at the end of a single, long, arching stem to form a cluster, 3-5" (7.5-12.5 cm) long; each flower is made up of 3 petals and 3 petal-like sepals, giving the appearance of 6 petals

Leaf: oval, stalkless leaves, 3-6" (7.5-15 cm) long, hairy underneath with heavy parallel veining

Fruit: a cluster of waxy red berries

Bloom: spring, summer

Cycle/Origin: perennial, native

Habitat: deciduous woods

Range: throughout

Stan's Notes: A spike flower cluster at the end of the stem of the False Solomon's Seal distinguishes it from Smooth Solomon's Seal (pg. 67), whose flowers hang beneath the stem. This woodland perennial grows on the forest floor from an elongated horizontal rootstock. Its waxy red berries are not edible. The common name Solomon's Seal comes from a scar, which resembles the seal of King Solomon, left on the rootstock by the growing stem.

CLUSTER TYPE	FLOWER TYPE	LEAF TYPE	LEAF ATTACHMENT	FRUIT
		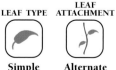		
Spike	**Regular**	**Simple**	**Alternate**	**Berry**

WHITE WATER LILY
Nymphaea odorata

Family: Water-Lily (Nymphaeaceae)

Height: aquatic

Flower: floating white flowers, 3-6" (7.5-15 cm) wide, made up of many pointed petals surrounding a yellow center

Leaf: round or heart-shaped, deeply notched, toothless, shiny, green, floating leaves, 5-12" (12.5-30 cm) wide

Bloom: summer, fall

Cycle/Origin: perennial, native

Habitat: small lakes, channels, bays

Range: throughout

Stan's Notes: Unlike the American Lotus (pg. 397), the White Water Lily's leaves float directly on the water's surface. This common pond lily requires quiet water because it is rooted to the lake or pond bottom. Its roots produce large tubers that are often eaten by muskrats. Its stems and leaves have air channels that trap air to keep the plant afloat. Flowers open on sunny days and close at night and on cloudy days. A third species of water lily found in Minnesota is the Small White Water Lily (*N. tetragona*); it occurs only in the far north and has white flowers half as large as the White Water Lily.

FLOWER TYPE	LEAF TYPE	LEAF ATTACHMENT
Regular	**Simple**	**Basal**

fruit

WILD CUCUMBER
Echinocystis lobata

Family: Gourd (Cucurbitaceae)

Height: 2-10' (60-300 cm); climbing vine

Flower: male flowers are showy, large, round clusters, 4-8" (10-20 cm) long; individual flowers, 6 thin petals, ½" (1 cm) wide, on erect stalks rising from a leaf joint; single female flower found at base of male flower stalk

Leaf: large maple-like leaves, each with 5 sharply divided lobes culminating in a point resembling a 5-pointed star

Fruit: single, large, pod-like container, 2" (5 cm) long, covered in rubbery spines that dries to a papery, skeleton-like, brown shell containing 4 seeds, each in its own chamber

Bloom: summer, fall

Cycle/Origin: annual, native

Habitat: wet, shade, deciduous woods

Range: throughout

Stan's Notes: Sometimes called Balsam Apple, this plant looks similar to the Bur Cucumber (pg. 241), but grows in wetter areas. It has long, curly forked tendrils and a square stem, and its leaves, flowers stalks and tendrils all arise from the same point on the vine. Its large fruit smells and tastes like cucumber, but will cause upset stomach and diarrhea. In flower it may appear as a mass of white flowers climbing over a shrub. The fruit dries to a papery, skeleton-like appearance, giving it the nickname, "Lace Pants."

CLUSTER TYPE	FLOWER TYPE	LEAF TYPE	LEAF ATTACHMENT	FRUIT
			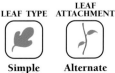	
Round	Regular	Simple Lobed	Alternate	Pod

COW PARSNIP
Heracleum maximum

Family: Carrot (Apiaceae)

Height: 4-9' (1.2-2.7 m)

Flower: a very large flat cluster, 4-8" (10-20 cm) wide, of white (sometimes purplish) flowers; individual flowers, ½" (1 cm) wide, have notched petals and are often larger toward the outer edges of the cluster

Leaf: an extremely large leaf, up to 12" (30 cm) wide, divided into 3 maple-like segments, 3-6" (7.5-15 cm) long; each is coarsely toothed and does not connect to one another; leafstalk is grossly swollen or inflated near the ridged and hollow main stem

Bloom: spring, summer

Cycle/Origin: perennial, native

Habitat: sun, moist areas along roads, lakes and streams

Range: throughout

Stan's Notes: A very tall, single-stemmed plant with large leaves and flat clusters of white flowers, the Cow Parsnip is often confused with the much smaller poisonous Water Hemlock (pg. 293). The Cow Parsnip's stem is grooved and hollow and, when the plant is bruised or cut, it emits a very rancorous odor. Look for the large inflated leafstalk (swelling) to help identify this plant, commonly found growing in wet or moist soil.

CLUSTER TYPE

Flat

FLOWER TYPE

Regular

LEAF TYPE

Simple Lobed

LEAF ATTACHMENT

Alternate

FLAT-TOPPED ASTER
Doellingeria umbellata

Family: Aster (Asteraceae)

Height: 1-6' (30-180 cm)

Flower: a flat cluster, 6-10" (15-25 cm) wide, of creamy white flower heads, ½-¾" (1-2 cm) wide; each flower head has 10-15 petals (ray flowers) with a yellow center (disk flowers)

Leaf: pointed, toothless, lance-shaped leaves, 3-6" (7.5-15 cm) long, alternate along the main stem

Bloom: summer, fall

Cycle/Origin: perennial, native

Habitat: wet, sun, edges of woods, swamps, prairies

Range: throughout

Stan's Notes: One of the first asters to bloom each summer, Flat-topped Aster grows a white flat cluster of flowers that attracts many insects. A single-stemmed plant with alternate leaves crowded along the stem, it grows in moist fields and along the edges of woods. Its center of yellow disk flowers turn purple with age. Its large flat cluster of flower heads make it one of the easiest asters to identify. Like other asters, Flat-topped Aster has composite flowers. Each flower is composed of white ray flowers and yellow disk flowers. Once the ray flowers are shed, the seedhead and flattened bracts look like tiny stars. A host plant for Pearl Crescent and Silvery Checkerspot butterfly caterpillars.

CLUSTER TYPE	FLOWER TYPE	LEAF TYPE	LEAF ATTACHMENT
	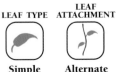		
Flat	**Composite**	**Simple**	**Alternate**

WHITE SWEET CLOVER
Melilotus alba

Family: Pea or Bean (Fabaceae)

Height: 3-6' (90-180 cm)

Flower: long spike clusters, 8" (20 cm) tall, of white pea-like flowers, ¼" (.6 cm) long; each grows on a short stalk

Leaf: each leaf divides into 3 narrow, toothed, lance-shaped leaflets, ½-1" (1-2.5 cm) long

Fruit: egg-shaped pod

Bloom: spring, summer, fall

Cycle/Origin: annual or biennial, non-native

Habitat: wet or dry, sun, along roads, open fields

Range: throughout

Stan's Notes: A non-native plant introduced from Europe via Eurasia, White Sweet Clover was once grown as a hay crop, but has escaped and now grows throughout Minnesota along roads and fields. This plant, along with Yellow Sweet Clover, is a major source of nectar for the Honeybee to make honey. Seeds can lie dormant in soil for decades until soil is disturbed and seeds come to within 7" (18 cm) of the surface. The amount of light in the 7" (18 cm) of soil is enough to trigger germination.This very fragrant plant smells like vanilla when its leaves or flowers are crushed. The genus name, *Melilotus*, is Greek for "honey," referring to its use as a nectar source for bees. Nearly identical to the Yellow Sweet Clover (pg. 399), except for the flower color.

CLUSTER TYPE	FLOWER TYPE	LEAF TYPE	LEAF ATTACHMENT	FRUIT

Spike	**Irregular**	**Compound**	**Alternate**	**Pod**

CULVER'S ROOT
Veronicastrum virginicum

Family: Snapdragon (Scrophulariaceae)

Height: 3-5' (90-150 cm)

Flower: many white tube-shaped flowers, ¼" (.6 cm) long, form a tapering spike cluster that grows up to 10-12" (25-30 cm) long; individual flower tubes are made up of 4 fused petals

Leaf: slender, finely toothed, lance-shaped leaves, 2-6" (5-15 cm) long, whorl around each stem in groups of 3-7

Bloom: summer

Cycle/Origin: perennial, native

Habitat: prairies, meadows, fields, along railroad tracks

Range: throughout

Stan's Notes: A tall showy plant of native prairies, Culver's Root can still be found along railroad beds and roads. Used by American pioneers as a medicinal plant because its roots contain several toxic chemicals, and its sap contains a strong emetic and laxative. This member of the Snapdragon family is closely related to several cultivated garden plants. Some plants have only one spike, while others have three to five. Bees are especially attracted to its flowers.

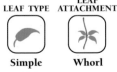

CLUSTER TYPE	FLOWER TYPE	LEAF TYPE	LEAF ATTACHMENT
Spike	Tube	Simple	Whorl

BLACK MEDICK
Medicago lupulina

Family: Pea or Bean (Fabaceae)

Height: 1-2" (2.5-5 cm)

Flower: many tiny, yellow flowers, ⅛" (.3 cm) long, form a small round cluster, ¼" (.6 cm) long; each cluster consists of 20-25 individual flowers and sits at the end of a thin stalk

Leaf: typical clover-type leaves, ¼-½" (.6-1 cm) long, made up of 3 round leaflets, each with fine teeth along the edge, and a single, tiny, sharp point at the end

Fruit: tiny, twisted black seedpod, ⅛-¼" (.3-.6 cm) long

Bloom: spring, summer

Cycle/Origin: annual, non-native

Habitat: dry, sun, lawns, along roads

Range: throughout

Stan's Notes: A very low-growing and small prostrate plant most often seen growing in lawns or along roads, Black Medick is a native of Eurasia that has spread throughout Minnesota. Its stems are covered with short, soft, whitish hairs, giving them a fuzzy appearance. It is considered a weed because it grows in lawns. Very common but so small it is often overlooked. The Medick seeds are a very important food for migrant sparrows in the fall.

CLUSTER TYPE	LEAF TYPE	LEAF ATTACHMENT	FRUIT

Round	Compound	Alternate	Pod

313

LEAFY SPURGE
Euphorbia esula

Family: Spurge (Euphorbiaceae)

Height: 1-2' (30-60 cm)

Flower: flat cluster, 2-3" (5-7.5 cm) wide, of 15-25 yellow green flowers; individual flower is actually 2 large colored bracts that surround an extremely small green flower, 1/8" (.3 cm) wide

Leaf: narrow lance-shaped leaves, 1-3" (2.5-7.5 cm) long, lacking a leaf stem; milky sap oozes when broken

Bloom: spring, summer

Cycle/Origin: perennial, non-native

Habitat: dry, sun, fields, along roads, in disturbed soils

Range: throughout

Stan's Notes: A very aggressive European import officially considered a noxious weed in Minnesota. A colored, petal-like bract, not actual petals, characterizes this and other members of the Spurge family (the Christmas Poinsettia is a good example of petal-like red bracts, which are not true flowers). Its stems and leaves contain a white, very sticky, milky sap, and it spreads along a horizontal, underground root system (rhizome). If its rootstock is cut up in an attempt to eradicate it, each root section will grow into a new plant. Because of this, special beetles are now being released to eat it in an attempt to control its aggressive growth. The common name, "Spurge," comes from the Latin *expurgare* (to purge), describing the laxative properties of this poisonous plant.

CLUSTER TYPE

Flat

LEAF TYPE

Simple

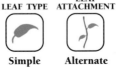

LEAF ATTACHMENT

Alternate

BIRDS-FOOT TREFOIL
Lotus corniculatus

Family: Pea or Bean (Fabaceae)

Height: 6-24" (15-60 cm)

Flower: showy, yellow, pea-like flowers, ½" (1 cm) long, clustered in a large mass of flowers

Leaf: a 5-part compound leaf made up of 3-part upper clover-like leaflets and 2 lower leaflets at the stalk base

Fruit: slender, 3-5, parted, pea-like pods, about 1" (2.5 cm) long

Bloom: spring, summer, fall

Cycle/Origin: perennial, non-native

Habitat: dry, sunny, old fields, especially along roads

Range: throughout

Stan's Notes: A non-native plant introduced from Europe as a cultivated forage crop, the Birds-foot Trefoil was widely planted for erosion control along newly constructed roads. It can be very aggressive and take over disturbed soils very quickly. Its flowers start out a bright lemon yellow but turn reddish orange with age. Its common name refers in part to its seedpods, which together look like a bird's foot, and its leaves, which mistakenly appear to grow in threes; hence "tre" foil. It is one of approximately 60 species of trefoil, most found in the western U.S.. A nectar source for European Skipper and Sulphur butterflies.

FLOWER TYPE	LEAF TYPE	LEAF ATTACHMENT	FRUIT
Irregular	**Compound**	**Alternate**	**Pod**

YELLOW WOOD SORREL
Oxalis stricta

Family: Wood Sorrel (Oxalidaceae)

Height: 6-15" (15-37.5 cm)

Flower: 1 to many, bright yellow flowers, ½" (1 cm) wide, made up of 5 petals

Leaf: each leaf is divided into 3 heart-shaped leaflets, resembling a compound clover leaf

Fruit: narrow pod-like capsule, ½" (1 cm) long, standing upright on a thin stalk

Bloom: spring, summer, fall

Cycle/Origin: annual, native

Habitat: dry, sun, disturbed soils, gardens, along roads

Range: throughout

Stan's Notes: Also called Oxalis, Yellow Wood Sorrel is a weak-stemmed plant that often grows unwanted in gardens. The leaves, stems and seedpods of this edible plant have a sour taste (the genus name, *Oxalis*, is Greek for "sour," and children often call it Sour Grass). Caution should be taken, however, as the plant contains oxalic acid which can cause upset stomach. Because it contains a high concentration of Vitamin C, phosphorus and potassium, Yellow Wood Sorrel has been used as a folk medicine to treat many ailments. It produces many seeds which become food for juncos and sparrows.

FLOWER TYPE	LEAF TYPE	LEAF ATTACHMENT	FRUIT
Regular	Compound	Alternate	Pod

DOWNY YELLOW VIOLET
Viola pubescens

Family: Violet (Violaceae)

Height: 8-16" (20-40 cm)

Flower: several yellow flowers per plant; individual flower, ¾" (2 cm) wide, made up of 5 petals with several dark purple veins; each flower grows on its own stalk

Leaf: hairy heart-shaped leaves with round or scalloped teeth, alternately attached to the main stem

Bloom: spring, summer

Cycle/Origin: perennial, native

Habitat: wet, cool, shade, deciduous woods

Range: throughout

Stan's Notes: One of the few "stalked" violets, the Yellow Downy Violet's flowers arise on stalks that originate from a leaf attachment (axis) rather than the more typical basal flower stalk. Its stalks (and to a lesser degree, its leaves) are covered with "down" hairs, hence the common name. This hairiness also helps to differentiate it from the many other yellow violets. The purple veins are guidelines or "come-ons" for pollinating insects to get to the pollen and nectar. The seed capsule acts like a shotgun. As the capsule dries, it compresses, bursts and shoots the seeds in all directions.

FLOWER TYPE	LEAF TYPE	LEAF ATTACHMENT
Irregular	Simple	Alternate

GROUND CHERRY
Physalis heterophylla

Family: Nightshade (Solanaceae)

Height: 6½-12" (16-30 cm)

Flower: pale yellow, bell-shaped flowers, ¾" (1.9 cm) long, with dark purple centers, arise from the upper stem's leafstalk junctions (axis) and hang straight down; 5 petals fuse together to form the bell-shaped flowers

Leaf: lance-shaped leaves, up to 2½" (6.3 cm) long, with infrequent teeth, sit on a short leafstalk

Fruit: inflated, green, papery husk harbors a green berry that turns orange to yellow orange when mature

Bloom: spring, summer

Cycle/Origin: perennial, native

Habitat: dry, sun, prairies, old fields

Range: throughout

Stan's Notes: The Ground Cherry's unique inflated fruit looks like the fruit of the Chinese Lantern (*P. alkekengi*), a garden plant with white flowers and orange fruit. Its leaves resemble those of its close relative, the tomato. Once used as a medicinal plant, the Ground Cherry's ripe fruit is edible, but its unripe green fruit is toxic, and grazing animals that eat it have been poisoned. Its leaf shape gives it its other common name, the Lance-leaved Ground Cherry. A host plant for the caterpillars of Sphinx Moths (also known as Hummingbird Moths).

FLOWER TYPE
Bell

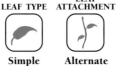
LEAF TYPE
Simple

LEAF ATTACHMENT
Alternate

FRUIT
Berry

CANADA HAWKWEED
Hieracium kalmii

Family: Aster (Asteraceae)

Height: 1-3' (30-90 cm)

Flower: 4-10 bright yellow, dandelion-like flowers, ¾-1" (2-2.5 cm) wide, grow on a single stalk and only open a few at a time; a composite flower, it is made up of 20-30 individual ray flowers, lacking the center disk flowers

Leaf: coarse-toothed, linear basal leaves, 2-5" (5-12.5 cm) long, stem leaves 1" (2.5 cm) long (cauline) stalkless with sharp teeth

Bloom: summer

Cycle/Origin: perennial, non-native

Habitat: dry, sun, fields, along roads, sandy soils, pastures

Range: northern and eastern regions of the state, mostly along the North Shore of Lake Superior

Stan's Notes: This is one of seven species of Hawkweed that grow in Minnesota, and it is often hard to correctly identify each species. This single-stemmed plant holds up to ten flowers that close at night and on cloudy days. After pollination, its flower heads produce a dandelion-like silk to carry away the seeds, further spreading the plant. It mainly reproduces by spreading leafy runners (stolon) across the ground. The name "Hawkweed" came from the mistaken belief that hawks ate the flowers to improve their vision.

FLOWER TYPE	LEAF TYPE	LEAF ATTACHMENT	LEAF ATTACHMENT
Composite	Simple	Alternate	Basal

WILD OATS
Uvularia sessilifolia

Family: Lily (Liliaceae)

Height: 6-12" (15-30 cm)

Flower: usually 1, but sometimes 2, pale yellow, drooping, bell flowers, 1" (2.5 cm) long; individual flower has 6 petals, (actually 3 petals and 3 petal-like sepals) at the end of a forked stem

Leaf: lance-shaped leaves, 1-3" (2.5-7.5 cm) long, light green with a whitish underside; stalkless

Bloom: spring

Cycle/Origin: perennial, native

Habitat: deciduous woods

Range: throughout, except for the southwestern corner

Stan's Notes: A common woodland perennial, similar to the Large-flowered Bellwort (pg. 345), Wild Oats is sometimes called Sessile-leaved Bellwort. "Sessile" refers to the fact that the leaves lack leafstalks. "Bellwort" refers to the shape of the flower: "bell" and "wort" mean common. Usually a single-stemmed plant that forks into two stalks with a flower at the end of only one stalk. Once thought to have medicinal properties to treat throat disorders because the droopy flowers resemble the uvula, the soft lobe hanging in the back of your throat (genus name, *Uvularia*).

FLOWER TYPE	LEAF TYPE	LEAF ATTACHMENT
Bell	**Simple**	**Alternate**

COMMON ST. JOHNSWORT
Hypericum perforatum

Family: St. Johnswort (Hypericaceae)

Height: 1-3' (30-90 cm)

Flower: an open cluster of up to 20 bright yellow flowers, 1" (2.5 cm) wide, each with 5 petals with black dots on each petal edge (margin); many long and thin protruding flower parts (stamens)

Leaf: narrow, stalkless lance-shaped leaves, 1-2" (2.5-5 cm) long, with many translucent dots

Bloom: summer, fall

Cycle/Origin: perennial, non-native

Habitat: dry, sun, fields, roadsides, disturbed soils

Range: throughout

Stan's Notes: A non-native plant of roadsides and fields, Common St. Johnswort is a highly branched plant. The dots on its leaves, best seen if a leaf is held up to light, are actually oil-filled glands. Introduced from Europe, its common name comes from the fact that the flower blooms on or near June 24, St. John's Day ("wort" means "common"). It is often used in folk medicine to treat eye problems and respiratory illnesses, and many of these medicinal uses have been recently revived. Dried leaves were also a talisman against witches and thunder, and a tea made of the leaves was used to relieve depression.

FLOWER TYPE	LEAF TYPE	LEAF ATTACHMENT
Regular	Simple	Opposite

GUMWEED
Grindelia squarrosa

Family: Aster (Asteraceae)

Height: 6-36" (15-90 cm)

Flower: 3-20 yellow flower heads, 1" (2.5 cm) wide, with 20 or more short petals (ray flowers) that surround a central yellow disk (disk flowers); green, outward-curling bracts surround each flower head and exude a sticky gum-like resin

Leaf: simple oval leaves, 1-2½" (2.5-6 cm) long, often with wavy or curled edges and coarse teeth, usually lacking a leafstalk

Bloom: summer, fall

Cycle/Origin: perennial, native

Habitat: dry, sun, fields, along roads, disturbed soils

Range: throughout

Stan's Notes: Also called Gum Plant, Sticky Heads or Tarweed, its many common names refer to the sticky resin secreted from the bracts that surround each flower head. Gumweed resin will stain your hands and has been used by many cultures as a medicine for everything from asthma to healing wounds. A plant of the American West that has now expanded its range eastward, Gumweed is one of the first plants to grow after construction or in heavily grazed fields, and is commonly seen along roads and railroads. Its flower heads are commonly used in arrangements of dried flowers.

FLOWER TYPE	LEAF TYPE	LEAF ATTACHMENT
Composite	Simple	Alternate

JEWELWEED
Impatiens pallida

Family: Touch-me-not (Balsaminaceae)

Height: 3-5' (90-150 cm)

Flower: yellow tube flowers, 1" (2.5 cm) long, with a few dark reddish brown spots deep within their throats; each flower has a large open mouth that leads to a long, thin, downward-curved spur, containing nectar

Leaf: sharply toothed oval leaves, 1-4" (2.5-10 cm) long, on a short leafstalk

Fruit: thin, banana-shaped, green pod-like container

Bloom: summer

Cycle/Origin: annual, native

Habitat: wet, shade, wetlands, along streams

Range: southern half of the state

Stan's Notes: Also called Pale Touch-me-not, the Jewelweed is so named because water droplets on its leaves shine like tiny jewels. This tall annual plant of wet areas has nearly translucent stems that contain a slippery juice that can be used to soothe the sting from nettles or Poison Ivy. Its long, thin ripe seedpods explode when touched, throwing seeds in all directions. This action provides its alternative common name, Touch-me-not. A similar species, Spotted Touch-me-not (pg. 81), has orange flowers with many dark red spots. A great flower to attract hummingbirds.

FLOWER TYPE

Tube

LEAF TYPE

Simple

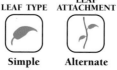

LEAF ATTACHMENT

Alternate

FRUIT

Pod

SWAMP BUTTERCUP
Ranunculus hispidus

Family: Buttercup (Ranunculaceae)

Height: 1-3' (30-90 cm)

Flower: showy yellow flowers, 1" (2.5 cm) wide, grow on erect stalks above the leaves; individual flowers have 5 round, bright yellow petals

Leaf: distinct 3-lobed leaves, 3-4" (7.5-10 cm) wide, grow on long stalks; each lobe is again divided into 3 lobes with sharp teeth

Fruit: cluster of green, beaked, seedpods; each pod contains a winged seed

Bloom: spring, summer

Cycle/Origin: perennial, native

Habitat: wet, shade, deciduous woods, meadows, along streams, neglected gardens

Range: throughout

Stan's Notes: A large robust plant with long, hollow, arching stems, Swamp Buttercup often spreads by rooting where its stems touch the ground, eventually forming large clusters. The plant is very deeply rooted and difficult to remove if grown in a garden. Swamp Buttercup's common name comes from its habit of growing in wet soils and the "cup" shape of its "buttery" yellow flowers. Its flowers produce much pollen but little nectar, so it attracts pollen-eating beetles, flies and bees.

FLOWER TYPE

Regular

LEAF TYPE

Simple Lobed

LEAF ATTACHMENT

Alternate

FRUIT

Pod

YELLOW TROUT LILY
Erythronium americanum

Family: Lily (Liliaceae)

Height: 5-10" (12.5-25 cm)

Flower: each stalk produces a single hanging yellow flower, 1" (2.5 cm) wide; each flower has 6 backward-curving petals (actually 3 petals and 3 petal-like sepals)

Leaf: a pair of elliptical, pointed basal leaves, up to 8" (20 cm) long, with brownish purple spots and streaks, giving it a mottled look

Fruit: egg-shaped, green pod-like capsule

Bloom: spring

Cycle/Origin: perennial, native

Habitat: dry, deciduous woods

Range: eastern edge of the state north to Duluth

Stan's Notes: Also called Dogtooth Violet, Yellow Trout Lily is a member of the Lily family, not a violet ("Dogtooth" refers to the tooth shape of its underground bulb). The common name "Trout" comes from its mottled leaves, which resemble the coloring of a Brown Trout. One of the most common spring wildflowers found carpeting deciduous forest floors, the Yellow Trout Lily reproduces mostly by underground bulbs. It may take up to seven years for a plant to be mature enough to flower. Nearly identical to the White Trout Lily (pg. 219), except for the flower color.

FLOWER TYPE

Bell

LEAF TYPE

Simple

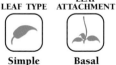

LEAF ATTACHMENT

Basal

FRUIT

Pod

PARTRIDGE PEA
Chamaecrista fasciculata

Family: Pea or Bean (Fabaceae)

Height: 1-2' (30-60 cm)

Flower: a row of yellow flowers, each flower about 1-1½" (2.5-4 cm) wide, grows along the main stem at each leaf attachment; each flower is made up of 5 teardrop-shaped petals, 5 green pointed sepals and a dark red center (stamens); the 4 upper petals have a dark red base

Leaf: compound leaves, 2-3" (5-7.5 cm) long, attach alternately along the erect main stem; each leaf is made up of 20-30 oval leaflets, ½" (1 cm) long

Fruit: flat, thin, hairy pod-like container, similar to that of the common garden pea

Bloom: summer, fall

Cycle/Origin: annual, native

Habitat: dry, sun, prairies, sandy soils, along roads

Range: southern half of the state

Stan's Notes: Partridge Pea is a common annual of native prairies throughout the southern half of the state. Does not have the characteristic pea flowers–resembles them only in that one petal is slightly larger than the other four and one of those is often curved. Its leaves fold up in direct sunlight, hence its other common name, Sensitive Pea.

FLOWER TYPE	LEAF TYPE	LEAF ATTACHMENT	FRUIT
Irregular	**Compound**	**Alternate**	**Pod**

MARSH MARIGOLD
Caltha palustris

Family: Buttercup (Ranunculaceae)

Height: 1-2' (30-60 cm)

Flower: many round, green-and-yellow buds open to become 5-9 bright yellow petals (actually sepals), 1-1½" (2.5-4 cm) wide

Leaf: round, toothless basal leaves, 2-7" (5-18 cm) wide, with long stalks and a deep notch where the stalk attaches; upper leaves stalkless, on the stem (cauline), 1-2" (2.5-5 cm) wide

Bloom: spring

Cycle/Origin: perennial, native

Habitat: wet, sun, along ponds, streams, lakes

Range: throughout

Stan's Notes: Also called Cowslip, the Marsh Marigold is well known for its bright yellow flowers that bloom very early in the spring. This wildflower grows in or along quiet waterways, such as streams and ponds. The genus name, *Caltha*, comes from the Latin word for "cup," and describes the plant's upturned petal-like sepals that form a shallow cup. The name "Marigold" comes from an Anglo-Saxon word meaning "marsh-gold." However, while the name is certainly a reasonable description of this plant, the Marsh Marigold is not a true marigold, but a type of buttercup. It is said the common name comes from the fact that the plant grew on the hummocks and cows slipped on it when they went to the stream to drink.

FLOWER TYPE	LEAF TYPE	LEAF ATTACHMENT	LEAF ATTACHMENT

Regular	Simple	Alternate	Basal

COMMON DANDELION
Taraxacum officinale

Family: Aster (Asteraceae)

Height: 2-18" (5-45 cm)

Flower: what appears to be 1 large yellow flower, 1½" (4 cm), is actually a composite of many tiny flowers clustered together

Leaf: a rosette of simple basal leaves with deep lobes and sharp teeth

Bloom: spring, summer, fall

Cycle/Origin: perennial, non-native

Habitat: dry, sun, lawns, fields

Range: throughout

Stan's Notes: This non-native perennial is responsible for much water contamination, as people treat lawns with chemicals to eradicate it. In French, *dent-de-lion* refers to the teeth of its leaf edge, resembling the teeth of a lion. Its flowers open in the morning and close in the afternoon. Globe-like seed heads have soft hair-like bristles that resemble tiny parachutes to carry the seeds away on the wind. The Red-seeded Dandelion is the other species of Dandelion in Minnesota. Originally brought from Eurasia as a food crop, its leaves taste bitter but offer high vitamin and mineral content, and its long taproot can be roasted and ground for a coffee substitute.

FLOWER TYPE	LEAF TYPE	LEAF ATTACHMENT
Composite	Simple Lobed	Basal

LARGE-FLOWERED BELLWORT
Uvularia grandiflora

Family: Lily (Liliaceae)

Height: 10-20" (25-50 cm)

Flower: drooping, pale yellow, bell flowers, 1-2" (2.5-5 cm) long, that appear to be weak and dehydrated; individual flowers have 6 petals

Leaf: long, pointed, lance-shaped, drooping leaves, 1-3" (2.5-7.5 cm) long; the stem passes through the base of the leaf as they alternate along the main stem

Bloom: spring

Cycle/Origin: perennial, native

Habitat: wet, shade, deciduous woods

Range: throughout

Stan's Notes: A single-stemmed plant that forks near the top into arching stems, the Large-flowered Bellwort has one to three drooping yellow flowers per stem. It grows in clumps containing up to several individual plants along horizontal underground roots (rhizomes), and its leaves have whitish downy hair underneath. The genus name, *Uvularia,* translates to "wood daffodil," and refers to its yellow daffodil-like color. The Large-flowered Bellwort is one of only two species of Bellwort in Minnesota (six species grow in eastern North America). Wild Oats (pg. 327), looks similar but has a white flower. An attractive wildflower for a shade garden.

FLOWER TYPE	LEAF TYPE	LEAF ATTACHMENT	LEAF ATTACHMENT
Bell	Simple	Alternate	Perfoliate

SNEEZEWEED
Helenium autumnale

Family: Aster (Asteraceae)

Height: 3-5' (90-150 cm)

Flower: a cluster of up to 100 flower heads per plant; each flower head, 1-2" (2.5-5 cm) wide, has 10-15 bright yellow, wedge-shaped petals (ray flowers), each tipped with 3 lobes; its characteristic yellow-green center of disk flowers is round and protrudes like a ball

Leaf: narrow, lance-shaped, stalkless leaves, ½-1" (1-2.5 cm) wide and 3-6" (7.5-15 cm) long, with widely spaced teeth; the edge of the leaf's base forms "wings" that extend down the main stem

Bloom: summer, fall

Cycle/Origin: perennial, native

Habitat: wet, sun, swamps, wet meadows and prairies, or along streams

Range: throughout, except for the Arrowhead Region

Stan's Notes: Sneezeweed often grows in a large dense clump with many flowers. Its round flower heads and unusually long leaf base ("wings") help to identify this member of the Aster family. Sneezeweed reportedly makes farm animals ill if eaten, and its dried leaves were once used as snuff (hence its common name). A similar species, Purple-headed Sneezeweed (*H. flexuosum*), has a dark brown-to-purple flower center and is found in dry fields and prairies.

FLOWER TYPE	LEAF TYPE	LEAF ATTACHMENT
Composite	Simple	Alternate

THIN-LEAVED CONEFLOWER
Rudbeckia triloba

Family: Aster (Asteraceae)

Height: 2-5' (60-150 cm)

Flower: each plant is covered with 50-100 yellow flower heads, 1-2" (2.5-5 cm) wide, each flower is made up of 6-10 yellow petals (ray flowers) surrounding a brown cone-shaped center (disk flowers)

Leaf: lower leaves, 3-4" (7.5-10 cm) long, have 3 pointed lobes; upper leaves, 2-3" (5-7.5 cm) long, are simple and coarsely toothed

Bloom: fall

Cycle/Origin: annual or biennial, native

Habitat: dry, sun, fields, along roads, prairies

Range: southern half of the state

Stan's Notes: Sometimes grown as a garden plant for its late autumn burst of color, Thin-leaved Coneflower can grow up to 100 flower heads per plant. Each petal (ray flower) is grooved along its length with a narrow notch at the tip. Look for the three-lobed lower leaves and simple upper leaves to help identify this wildflower, which looks like a miniature Black-eyed Susan (pg. 359).

FLOWER TYPE
Composite

LEAF TYPE
Simple

LEAF TYPE
Simple Lobed

LEAF ATTACHMENT
Alternate

ZIGZAG GOLDENROD
Solidago flexicaulis

Family: Aster (Asteraceae)

Height: 1-3' (30-90 cm)

Flower: several round clusters, 1-2" (2.5-5 cm) wide, of yellow flower heads located at each of the leaf joints (axis); individual flowers, ¼" (.6 cm) wide, have only 3-4 petals (ray flowers)

Leaf: pointed, coarse-toothed, oval leaves, 1-3" (2.5-7.5 cm) long, alternate along the stem; leaves are dark green with a short leafstalk

Bloom: fall

Cycle/Origin: perennial, native

Habitat: dry, shade, in clearings and along the edges of deciduous woods

Range: throughout, except for the extreme northern counties

Stan's Notes: Zigzag Goldenrod is a woodland goldenrod with one to three erect stems per plant. The stems bend back and forth between each leaf attachment, hence the common name, "Zigzag" (this characteristic is sometimes hard to see, and is most obvious between the upper leaves). One of the few goldenrods with flower clusters located at each leaf joint rather than spikes near the top of the plant. The only goldenrod to grow in the forest. A nice plant for the shady flower garden.

CLUSTER TYPE
Round

FLOWER TYPE
Composite

LEAF TYPE
Simple

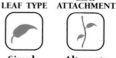
LEAF ATTACHMENT
Alternate

GOAT'S BEARD
Tragopogon dubius

Family: Aster (Asteraceae)

Height: 1-3' (30-90 cm)

Flower: a single large, yellow, dandelion-like flower head, 1-2½" (2.5-6 cm) wide, of many petals (ray flowers) but no center disk flowers; its stalk is swollen just below the flower head

Leaf: simple, grass-like leaves, 1' (30 cm) long and just ½" (1 cm) wide, clasp the stem

Bloom: spring, summer

Cycle/Origin: biennial, non-native

Habitat: dry, sun, fields, along roads

Range: throughout

Stan's Notes: Sometimes called Yellow Goatsbeard, this European import looks like a large dandelion and is common along roads and in open fields. Its large yellow flower head, which turns to face the sun, opens only on sunny mornings and closes by noon, which has led to another common name, Johnny-go-to-bed-at-noon (several other plants share this moniker). Its long taproots can be dug and roasted as a coffee substitute, and the entire plant produces a sticky, milky sap. The seed head looks like a giant dandelion plume or like an old gray goat's beard, and children often call its mature flower heads "blow balls." Some people spray these seed heads with hairspray and use them in dried flower arrangements.

FLOWER TYPE	LEAF TYPE	LEAF ATTACHMENT	LEAF ATTACHMENT
Composite	Simple	Alternate	Clasping

GRAY-HEADED CONEFLOWER
Ratibida pinnata

Family: Aster (Asteraceae)

Height: 3-7' (90-210 cm)

Flower: up to 15 droopy yellow petals (ray flowers) surround a thimble-shaped cone (disk flower), 2-2½" (5-6 cm) tall, that is always taller than it is wide; 10-25 very showy flower heads per plant, each on an individual stalk

Leaf: highly divided leaves, up to 7" (18 cm) long, with many thin, coarsely toothed lobes; its basal leaves have long stalks up to 7" (18 cm) and its stalkless, undivided, upper leaves (cauline) become smaller near the top

Bloom: summer

Cycle/Origin: perennial, native

Habitat: dry, sun, along roads, prairies

Range: throughout, mostly in the southern half of the state

Stan's Notes: A magnificently tall plant of roadsides and native prairies, the Gray-headed Coneflower's tall, thin, hairy stems support striking yellow flowers with relaxed or droopy petals. After pollination, the cone (disk flower) dries to a light gray color and smells strongly of spice when crushed. Also called Yellow Coneflower.

FLOWER TYPE	LEAF TYPE	LEAF ATTACHMENT
Composite	Simple Lobed	Alternate

WINTER CRESS
Barbarea vulgaris

Family: Mustard (Brassicaceae)

Height: 1-2' (30-60 cm)

Flower: several spike clusters, 2-3" (5-7.5 cm) long, of bright yellow flowers; individual flowers, ¼" (.6 cm) wide, are made up of 4 petals that form a cross

Leaf: lower leaves have long stalks, 3-5" (7.5-12.5 cm), with up to 5 lobes, the end or terminal lobe being the largest; coarsely toothed, upper stem leaves (cauline) often clasp the stem

Fruit: thin, erect, pod-like containers split lengthwise into 2 curled sides to release many tiny black seeds

Bloom: spring, fall

Cycle/Origin: biennial, non-native

Habitat: wet, sun, open fields, along roads or railroad tracks

Range: throughout

Stan's Notes: Winter Cress is one of the first wildflowers to bloom each spring, often while snow remains on the ground, hence its common name (it also blooms again in late autumn). A favorite of deer, it is one of the first green "deer foods" in the spring. Its tiny black seeds are very hot and peppery, and have been used as a pepper substitute; the plant itself has been used as a poultice to treat wounds in folk medicine. A member of the Mustard family (but not a true mustard), Winter Cress has six stamen, four long and two short.

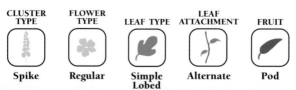

CLUSTER TYPE	FLOWER TYPE	LEAF TYPE	LEAF ATTACHMENT	FRUIT
Spike	Regular	Simple Lobed	Alternate	Pod

BLACK-EYED SUSAN
Rudbeckia hirta

Family: Aster (Asteraceae)

Height: 1-3' (30-90 cm)

Flower: large flower head, 2-3" (5-7.5 cm) wide, with a brown button-like center (disk flowers) surrounded by 10-20 daisy-like yellow petals (ray flowers); 1 to numerous flower heads per plant

Leaf: slender, toothless, very hairy leaves, 2-7" (5-18 cm) long; each leafstalk clasps a hairy stem; winged leafstalk

Bloom: summer, fall

Cycle/Origin: perennial or biennial, native

Habitat: prairies, fields, dry, open, deciduous woods

Range: throughout

Stan's Notes: Also called the Brown-eyed Susan, look for three prominent veins on each leaf and a characteristic winged leafstalk clasping each erect, straight stem. Originally a native prairie plant, it is now found in just about any habitat, including along roads and in disturbed fields. Its seeds make an abundant food source for Goldfinches and House Finches. The species name, *hirta*, Latin for "hairy" or "rough," refers to the plant's hairy nature. Who "Susan" was remains unknown. A host plant for the black-with-orange striped, Silvery Checkerspot caterpillars. The caterpillars camouflage themselves with bits of the flower secured by silk while feeding on the brown centers of the Black-eyed Susan.

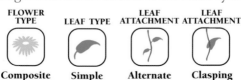

FLOWER TYPE	LEAF TYPE	LEAF ATTACHMENT	LEAF ATTACHMENT
Composite	Simple	Alternate	Clasping

GREEN-HEADED CONEFLOWER
Rudbeckia laciniata

Family: Aster (Asteraceae)

Height: 5-8' (1.5-2.4 cm)

Flower: each plant grows 20-50 large composite flower heads; individual flower heads, 2-3" (5-7.5 cm) wide, have 8-10 drooping yellow petals (ray flowers) surrounding a cone-shaped green center (disk flowers)

Leaf: lower leaves, 5-8" (12.5-20 cm) long, have 3-5 sharp lobes and coarse teeth; upper leaves, 2-3" (5-7.5 cm) long, are simple, coarsely toothed and nearly clasp the stem

Bloom: summer

Cycle/Origin: perennial, native

Habitat: wet, sun, fields, ditches, prairies

Range: throughout

Stan's Notes: A tall, robust, prairie perennial, Green-headed Coneflower grows in moist soils throughout the state. Look for its green center (cone) and drooping yellow petals–along with the lobed lower leaves and simple upper leaves–to help identify. Often seen growing in ditches or along roads and near old homesteads, it is also called Golden Glow. A good plant for a butterfly garden. Its flowers attract Monarchs and Fritillaries to feed on nectar.

FLOWER TYPE	LEAF TYPE	LEAF TYPE	LEAF ATTACHMENT
Composite	**Simple Lobed**	**Simple**	**Alternate**

YELLOW LADY'S SLIPPER
Cypripedium calceolus

Family: Orchid (Orchidaceae)

Height: 4-24" (10-60 cm)

Flower: 1-2 fragrant, muddy yellow flowers, 2-3" (5-7.5 cm) tall; a single large, inflated, yellow petal surrounded by 4 brownish purple (actually 2 petals and 2 petal-like sepals) twisted petals

Leaf: basal leaves, up to 8" (20 cm) long, with many deep parallel veins; smaller stem leaves (cauline) alternate and clasp the stem

Bloom: spring, summer

Cycle/Origin: perennial, native

Habitat: wet, shade, deciduous woods, swamps and bogs

Range: throughout, except the southwestern corner

Stan's Notes: The Yellow Lady's Slipper's genus name, *Cypridpedium,* can be broken into "*Cyprid,*" the original name for the goddess Venus, and "*pedium,*" Latin for "foot." Orchids are highly specialized plants needing their own special fungus growing on their roots to survive. This is why they are nearly impossible to transplant and should be enjoyed in the wild only. Orchid seeds are like specks of dust; they consist only of an embryo (no stored food). They depend on being invaded by a fungal hyphae to infuse the seeds with nutrients. This process takes several years before any roots or shoots develop. There are 42 species of native orchids in Minnesota.

FLOWER TYPE

LEAF TYPE

LEAF ATTACHMENT

LEAF ATTACHMENT

Irregular   Simple   Alternate   Basal

PRAIRIE DOCK
Silphium terebinthinaceum

Family: Aster (Asteraceae)

Height: 5-10' (1.5-3 m)

Flower: extremely tall stalk with up to 50 flower heads, 2-3" (5-7.5 cm) wide; individual flower head has up to 12-25 yellow petals (ray flowers), notched at the tip and surrounding a yellow cone (disk flowers)

Leaf: oval to spade-shaped (sometimes heart-shaped), very rough basal leaves, 16-24" (40-60 cm) long; leaves stand erect

Bloom: summer, fall

Cycle/Origin: perennial, native

Habitat: dry, sun, prairies

Range: southern quarter of the state

Stan's Notes: Prairie Dock's extremely large basal leaves make it an easily recognized prairie plant. Its flower stalks are leafless and stand well above any other plant in the prairie, and its stem contains a resinous sap. Prairie Dock is a long-lived plant because its deep roots make it very drought resistant. The common name, Dock, comes from its large dock-like leaves, which often orient themselves along a north/south axis to maximize the area of leaf surface facing the sun. One of the tallest and largest leaved plants of the prairie. Closely related to Cup Plant (pg. 381).

FLOWER TYPE	LEAF TYPE	LEAF ATTACHMENT
Composite	Simple	Basal

flower

PRICKLY PEAR
Opuntia macrorhiza

Family: Cactus (Cactaceae)

Height: 6-12" (15-30 cm)

Flower: several pale yellow flowers, 2-3" (5-7.5 cm) wide, of many petals, often with reddish centers

Leaf: broad, flat, fleshy pads, 2-4" (5-10 cm) wide and ½" (1 cm) thick, covered with tufts of sharp spines; join together by thick, spreading stalks

Fruit: round edible berry that starts out green and turns purple

Bloom: spring

Cycle/Origin: perennial, native

Habitat: dry, sun, native prairies, along roads

Range: southwestern corner of the state

Stan's Notes: Many consider it a contradiction that a cactus grows in Minnesota, but the Prickly Pear is one of two species of cacti that occur in the state; Brittle Prickly Pear (*O. fragilis*) also grows in Minnesota. Having been nearly eliminated from the state to protect livestock, it is now found in remnant native prairies in the southwestern portion of the state and along the Minnesota River Valley. The flowers are very pollen-rich and are frequently visited by flower flies, bees and beetles.

FLOWER TYPE

Regular

FRUIT

Berry

WILD PARSNIP
Pastinaca sativa

Family: Carrot (Apiaceae)

Height: 2-4' (60-120 cm)

Flower: 7-10 flat clusters, 2-3" (5-7.5 cm) wide, of many tiny yellow flowers, each only ¼" (.6 cm)

Leaf: compound leaf, 5-7" (12.5-18 cm) long, made up of 5-15 coarse-toothed, oval leaflets; its leafstalk has wide wings

Bloom: spring, summer

Cycle/Origin: biennial, non-native

Habitat: wet, sun, fields, roadsides

Range: throughout

Stan's Notes: Very common along wet roadsides and ditches, Wild Parsnip's many flowers often turn an entire roadside sunny yellow in the spring. A native of Eurasia, this biennial was introduced from Europe as a garden food crop. Its long taproot is too woody to be edible after the second year of growth. Now considered a weed in many places. Can cause photodermatitis if touched. Skin will blister and weep when exposed to sunlight after you touch the plant. Wear gloves and long sleeves and pants if you work among the plants. A host plant for the Black Swallowtail butterfly caterpillar.

CLUSTER TYPE	FLOWER TYPE	LEAF TYPE	LEAF ATTACHMENT
		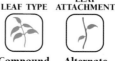	
Flat	Regular	Compound	Alternate

FALSE SUNFLOWER
Heliopsis helianthoides

Family: Aster (Asteraceae)

Height: 3-4' (90-120 cm)

Flower: bright yellow flower heads, 2-3" (5-7.5 cm) wide, with 20-30 petals (ray flowers) with a yellow center (disk flowers); only one flower head per stem

Leaf: coarsely toothed, lance-shaped leaves, 1-3" (2.5-7.5 cm) long, with a very short leafstalk, which makes the leaf appear to be clasping a smooth stem

Bloom: summer

Cycle/Origin: perennial, native

Habitat: dry, sun, fields, prairies

Range: throughout the state

Stan's Notes: Also called Ox-eye, the False Sunflower can be found throughout the state. Unlike true sunflowers, both the ray and disk flowers of the False Sunflower produce fruits. All flowers are borne on a single stalk, which is usually smooth (although some are rough). Look for a slight swelling in the stem just below the flower to help identify this perennial. A nice butterfly garden plant that is hardy and easy to grow.

FLOWER TYPE

Composite

LEAF TYPE

Simple

LEAF ATTACHMENT

Opposite

WOODLAND SUNFLOWER
Helianthus divaricatus

Family: Aster (Asteraceae)

Height: 3-7' (90-210 cm)

Flower: each plant produces 1-10 yellow flower heads, 2-4" (5-10 cm) wide, made up of 9-17 petals (ray flowers) that surround a yellow center (disk flowers)

Leaf: opposite, dark green, finely toothed, lance-shaped leaves, 3-8" (7.5-20 cm) long; leaves are rough to the touch and pale white underneath

Bloom: summer, fall

Cycle/Origin: perennial, native

Habitat: shade, along edges and clearings of deciduous woods

Range: throughout

Stan's Notes: Flower heads of the Woodland Sunflower have yellow petals and a yellow center, and its stems and leaves are rough (but occasionally smooth) to touch. Its upper leaves nearly clasp the stem while lower leaves have short leaf stems, and the plant usually grows in large clumps, each plant leaning toward available sunlight. The species name, *Helianthus,* comes from the Greek "*Helios*" (sun) and "*anthus*" (flower). A great producer of seeds for sparrows and finches.

FLOWER TYPE

Composite

LEAF TYPE

Simple

LEAF ATTACHMENT

Opposite

YELLOW FLAG IRIS
Iris pseudacorus

Family: Iris (Iridaceae)

Height: 2-3' (60-90 cm)

Flower: 1 to several large, yellow flowers, 2½-4" (6-10 cm) wide, rising on tall stiff stalks; individual flower has 6 petals, 3 large, backward-curving, petal-like sepals; 3 smaller, narrow, upright petals

Leaf: long, narrow, sword-like blades, 1" (2.5 cm) wide and 8-32" (20-80 cm) long, similar to garden irises

Fruit: large, green, round-ended pod, 1½-2" (4-5 cm), containing multiple seeds

Bloom: spring, summer

Cycle/Origin: perennial, non-native

Habitat: wet, sun or shade, edges of wetlands, lakes and rivers

Range: throughout

Stan's Notes: This European garden import now grows wild along water in clumps of tall, erect, sword-like leaves with many flowers. These clumps are created by toxic, horizontal underground roots (rhizome), which many cultures have used medicinally. Its largest petals are actually sepals. Insects pollinate by walking along the sepals, passing under the plant's male and female flower parts. The term "flag" from the Middle English *flagge*, means "rush" or "reed," and refers to the plant's leaves. "Iris" is derived from the Greek word for "rainbow," describing the wide range of flower color.

FLOWER TYPE	LEAF TYPE	LEAF ATTACHMENT	FRUIT
	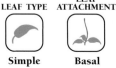		
Irregular	**Simple**	**Basal**	**Pod**

COMMON TANSY
Tanacetum vulgare

Family: Aster (Asteraceae)

Height: 2-4' (60-120 cm)

Flower: several flat, 2-4" (5-10 cm) wide, clusters of yellow, button-like composite flower heads; individual flower heads, ½" (1 cm) wide, look like common daisy flower heads without the white petals

Leaf: deeply divided, fern-like leaves, 4-8" (10-20 cm) long, with many sharp teeth

Bloom: summer, fall

Cycle/Origin: perennial, non-native

Habitat: dry, sun, along roads, disturbed soils

Range: throughout, especially along the North Shore of Lake Superior

Stan's Notes: A tall plant of roadsides and old fields (and sometimes grown in gardens), Common Tansy often forms dense patches of bright yellow flowers. Its leaves have a strong bitter or medicinal odor. The plant has been used in many folk remedies, although usually with poor results because the plant contains a toxic oil called tanacetum. The highly fragrant leaves are sometimes used as a substitute for sage in scented bags and pillows. A native of Europe, it can now be found around the world. Its composite flowers are composed only of disk flowers and look like little flat buttons.

CLUSTER TYPE	FLOWER TYPE	LEAF TYPE	LEAF ATTACHMENT

Flat	Composite	Simple Lobed	Alternate

COMPASS PLANT
Silphium laciniatum

Family: Aster (Asteraceae)

Height: 5-12' (1.5-3.6 m)

Flower: several bright yellow, sunflower-like flower heads, 3" (7.5 cm) wide, alternate along a tall stem; each flower head has up to 25 yellow petals (ray flowers) with a yellow center (disk flowers)

Leaf: basal leaves, 12-18" (30-45 cm) long, with deep narrow lobes, covered in fine hairs; each lobe is coarsely toothed and irregularly shaped

Bloom: summer, fall

Cycle/Origin: perennial native

Habitat: dry, sun, prairies, along railroad beds and roads

Range: southern half of the state

Stan's Notes: Closely related to all sunflowers, the Compass Plant is the tallest plant of the prairie, with some stems often reaching 12' (3.6 m). Its leaves, also some of the largest on the prairie, line up north to south to collect a maximum amount of sunlight, providing its common name. The plant oozes a sap that, when collected, makes a good chewing gum substitute. The Compass Plant's center disk flowers are often unable to produce seeds or be pollinated, and its long taproot makes it impossible to transplant. Finches are crazy for these seeds, picking them out before they even ripen.

FLOWER TYPE	LEAF TYPE	LEAF ATTACHMENT	LEAF ATTACHMENT
Composite	**Simple Lobed**	**Alternate**	**Basal**

CUP PLANT
Silphium perfoliatum

Family: Aster (Asteraceae)

Height: 3-6' (90-180 cm)

Flower: a multi-branched flower stalk with 10-30 sunflower-like yellow flower heads, 3-4" (7.5-10 cm) wide; each flower head has 24-30 bright yellow petals (ray flowers) with a light green-to-yellow center (disk flower); each flower is found on its own stalk

Leaf: lance-shaped leaves, 6-10" (15-25 cm) long, unite at the base to form a "cup" around the stem

Bloom: summer, fall

Cycle/Origin: perennial, native

Habitat: sun, prairie, along wetlands and streams

Range: southern half of the state

Stan's Notes: A robust plant of the prairie with a very unique leaf base (perfoliate), the Cup Plant's joined leaves form "cups" that hold rainwater, hence its common name. Birds take advantage of this water supply up to several days after a rainstorm. Tree frogs will also sit in the water that is captured in the cup. Only the yellow ray flowers (petals) produce seeds after pollination (the center disk flowers are sterile). Stems are often reddish in color, square, and smooth to the touch. In the fall, whole goldfinch families descend on the Cup Plant to harvest the seeds.

FLOWER TYPE	LEAF TYPE	LEAF ATTACHMENT

Composite	Simple	Perfoliate

STIFF GOLDENROD
Solidago rigida

Family: Aster (Asteraceae)

Height: 1-5' (30-150 cm)

Flower: many small, yellow flower heads, ⅓" (.8 cm) wide, form a flat cluster, 3-4" (7.5-10 cm) wide; each individual flower head has 7-10 yellow petals (ray flowers) and 20-30 center disk flowers

Leaf: blade-like, stalked basal leaves, 10" (25 cm) long, are rough to the touch and stand erect; leaves on the stem (cauline) are round and fleshy, alternate and clasping

Bloom: summer, fall

Cycle/Origin: perennial, native

Habitat: dry, sun, fields, prairies, along roads

Range: throughout

Stan's Notes: A common goldenrod of open fields and prairies, Stiff Goldenrod usually grows two or three stems that branch into flower heads near the top of the plant. Its main stem and leaves are hairy, making them rough to touch, and its basal leaves are stiff and stand erect, hence the common name. The plant's round fleshy leaves help to differentiate it from other species of goldenrod, making this goldenrod easier to identify. The flowers are an excellent source of nectar, attracting butterflies, bees, flower flies and beetles.

CLUSTER TYPE	FLOWER TYPE	LEAF TYPE	LEAF ATTACHMENT	LEAF ATTACHMENT	LEAF ATTACHMENT
Flat	Composite	Simple	Alternate	Basal	Clasping

YELLOW WATER LILY
Nuphar variegata

Family: Water-Lily (Nymphaeaceae)

Height: aquatic

Flower: floating, cup-shaped, yellow flowers, 3-5" (7.5-12.5 cm) wide, made up of 4 large yellow (sometimes green) petals, surrounded by up to 3 small petal-like sepals; the flowers stand up to several inches above the water surface.

Leaf: round or heart-shaped, deeply notched, toothless, shiny green floating leaves, 3-8" (7.5-20 cm) long

Bloom: summer, fall

Cycle/Origin: perennial, native

Habitat: small lakes, channels, bays

Range: throughout

Stan's Notes: Also called Bullhead Lily, the Yellow Water Lily is commonly found in small ponds, lakes and streams and is the only yellow pond lily in Minnesota. Unlike the American Lotus (pg. 397), its leaves float directly on the surface of the water. This common pond lily requires quiet water because it is rooted to the lake or pond bottom. Its roots produce large rhizomes that are often eaten by muskrats and beavers, and its stems and leaves have air channels that trap air to keep the plant afloat. Its flowers usually open only on sunny afternoons.

FLOWER TYPE	LEAF TYPE	LEAF ATTACHMENT
Regular	Simple	Basal

COMMON SUNFLOWER
Helianthus annuus

Family: Aster (Asteraceae)

Height: 3-10' (90-300 cm)

Flower: sunny yellow flower heads, 3-6" (7.5-15 cm) wide, each with 15-20 yellow petals (ray flowers), surround a large dark brown or purple center (disk flower); each plant has 2-20 flowers

Leaf: stiff, coarse-toothed triangular or heart-shaped leaves, 3-7" (7.5-18 cm) long, alternate along a very coarse stem

Bloom: summer, fall

Cycle/Origin: annual, native

Habitat: dry, sun, fields, along roads, open places

Range: throughout

Stan's Notes: A smaller, wild version of the Giant Sunflower, which is often cultivated in gardens and fields. Unlike the giant variety, the wild Common Sunflower usually branches several times but still produces many nutritious seeds. Used for food by many people in history, the Common Sunflower's seeds can be used in the making of flour, oil, and even medicine. It is often seen growing along highways where the seeds of maturing plants are dispersed along the road by wind created from passing cars and trucks. Sunflowers do not follow the sun, as widely believed. Their heads face the morning sun once they mature and begin to bloom, thus most flowers face east.

FLOWER TYPE

Composite

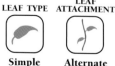

LEAF TYPE

Simple

LEAF ATTACHMENT

Alternate

BUTTER-AND-EGGS
Linaria vulgaris

Family: Snapdragon (Scrophulariaceae)

Height: 1-2' (30-60 cm)

Flower: a spike, 3-6" (7.5-15 cm) long, of irregular, yellow and orange pea-like flowers, 1" (2.5 cm) tall, each made of 5 petals fused together in a snapdragon-like flower; a thin spur below each flower contains nectar

Leaf: thin, pale, gray green, grass-like leaves, 1-2" (2.5-5 cm) long, sometimes set opposite near the base but alternate above

Bloom: spring, summer, fall

Cycle/Origin: perennial, non-native

Habitat: dry, sun, open fields, disturbed soils, along roads

Range: throughout

Stan's Notes: Butter-and-eggs was introduced from Europe, escaped from gardens and now grows throughout Minnesota. A two-toned flower whose orange part, known as the "honey guide," acts like a target to guide insects into the long spur of the flower, ensuring that the insect pollinates it before getting the nectar. It often grows in patches and reproduces along a horizontal underground root (rhizome), and is a favorite of the hummingbird-like Sphinx Moth. This plant takes its name from its yellow (butter) and orange (egg yolk) flowers. When its flower is pinched, it opens wide like a frog's mouth, providing its other common name, Toadflax.

CLUSTER TYPE	FLOWER TYPE	LEAF TYPE	LEAF ATTACHMENT
		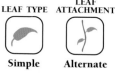	
Spike	Irregular	Simple	Alternate

CANADA GOLDENROD
Solidago canadensis

Family: Aster (Asteraceae)

Height: 2-5' (60-150 cm)

Flower: a mass of small individual yellow flower heads, ¼" (.6 cm) wide, arranged in large, arching, spike clusters, 3-9" (7.5-22.5 cm) tall; the tip of the tallest flower cluster nods to one side

Leaf: narrow, up to 6" (15 cm) long, rough to touch, sharp teeth along edges; fewer leaves near base of stem

Bloom: summer, fall

Cycle/Origin: perennial, native

Habitat: dry, sun, open fields, prairies

Range: throughout

Stan's Notes: This common plant, often seen in roadside patches, reproduces by sending up new plants from roots (clones), creating patches 8-30' (2.4-9.1 m) wide, excluding other plants from the site. There are over 100 types of goldenrod in North America and over 15 in Minnesota, all looking similar, thus difficult to identify. Most yellow autumn flowers are a type of goldenrod, and are often mistakenly blamed for hay fever. Only 1-2% of autumn airborne pollen is from goldenrod (most hay fever is caused by Giant Ragweed). Goldenrod is pollinated by insects, including beetles, ambush bugs, flies, midges and bees, which are attracted to the flower's abundant nectar. Goldenrod stems are often invaded by insect larvae (usually a solitary wasp or fly larvae), causing large swellings (galls).

CLUSTER TYPE	FLOWER TYPE	LEAF TYPE	LEAF ATTACHMENT
Spike	Composite	Simple	Alternate

GOLDEN ALEXANDERS
Zizia aurea

Family: Carrot (Apiaceae)

Height: 1-3' (30-90 cm)

Flower: tiny creamy yellow flowers, ¼" (.6 cm) wide, form flat clusters, 5-6" (12.5-15 cm) across

Leaf: a single (compound) leaf that divides into 3 stalks; each stalk with 3-7 narrow, coarse-toothed, pointed leaflets

Bloom: spring

Cycle/Origin: perennial, native

Habitat: wet, sun, ditches, along roads, moist fields, woods

Range: throughout

Stan's Notes: The Golden Alexanders is related to parsley and is part of the Carrot family, whose members share a similar flat-topped cluster of flowers called an umbel. Its stems are often tinged with red. Commonly seen in large patches in late spring along roads in wet ditches, it is often confused with Wild Parsnip (pg. 369), which also has a flat-topped cluster of yellow flowers. It is also related to Water Hemlock (pg. 293), a deadly plant of the same habitat with a flat cluster of white flowers. Was once used to heal wounds, and relieve fevers and syphilis.

CLUSTER TYPE	FLOWER TYPE	LEAF TYPE	LEAF ATTACHMENT
		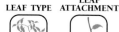	
Flat	Regular	Twice Compound	Alternate

EVENING PRIMROSE
Oenothera biennis

Family: Evening Primrose (Onagraceae)

Height: 2-5' (60-150 cm)

Flower: many pale yellow flowers, 1-2" (2.5-5 cm) tall, in a round cluster, 6-10" (15-25 cm) wide; individual flowers have 4 petals and an **X**-shaped center (stigma)

Leaf: narrow, lance-shaped leaves, 4-8" (10-20 cm) long, alternate along a hairy stem; leaves are rough to the touch and often tinged with red along the edge

Fruit: blunt-topped green pod-like container, ½-2" (1-5 cm) long, with lengthwise ridges

Bloom: summer, fall

Cycle/Origin: biennial, native

Habitat: dry, sun, prairies, along roads

Range: throughout

Stan's Notes: As a biennial, the Evening Primrose produces a low ring (rosette) of leaves in its first year, sending up a tall flower stalk in its second. Its flowers bloom starting at the bottom going up, opening a few at a time. The flowers open in the evening and last until about noon the next day before wilting, hence the common name. Its pods contain many seeds eaten by wildlife. Nearly ten other species of Evening Primrose are found in Minnesota and all but one have the unique **X**-shaped center (stigma) and yellow flowers. The flowers of this plant are pollinated by Sphinx Moths at night.

CLUSTER TYPE	FLOWER TYPE	LEAF TYPE	LEAF ATTACHMENT	FRUIT
		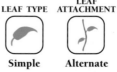		
Round	Regular	Simple	Alternate	Pod

fruit

AMERICAN LOTUS
Nelumbo lutea

Family: Water-Lily (Nymphaeaceae)

Height: aquatic

Flower: pale yellow, cup-shaped flowers, 6-10" (15-25 cm) wide; many large petals surround large yellow center; flowers stand up to 12" (30 cm) above water

Leaf: very large, round, toothless leaves, 1-2' (30-60 cm) wide, stand up to 12" (30 cm) above the water; edges are often upturned to form a shallow bowl

Fruit: round, green-turning-brown pod-like container with numerous acorn-like seeds; top has many openings (like swiss cheese) to release seeds

Bloom: summer, fall

Cycle/Origin: perennial, native

Habitat: small lakes, channels, bays

Range: southeastern corner of the state

Stan's Notes: The large round leaves and flower of this plant (perhaps the largest flower of Minnesota's wildflowers) stand well above the water, waving in the wind, distinguishing it from other water lilies. Its pale yellow flowers open only on sunny days, giving rise to the large seedpods often used in dried floral arrangements; the seeds within the head are edible. Like other water lilies, its roots are eaten by wildlife, and its seeds and roots were used as food by Native Americans. They also used the seeds for counters and dice in games.

FLOWER TYPE

Regular

LEAF TYPE

Simple

LEAF ATTACHMENT

Basal

FRUIT

Pod

YELLOW SWEET CLOVER
Melilotus officinalis

Family: Pea or Bean (Fabaceae)

Height: 3-6' (90-180 cm)

Flower: spike clusters, 8" (20 cm) long, of irregular, yellow flowers, ¼" (.6 cm) tall

Leaf: each leaf divides into 3 narrow, toothed lance-shaped leaflets, ½-1" (1-2.5 cm) long

Fruit: egg-shaped pod

Bloom: spring, summer, fall

Cycle/Origin: annual or biennial, non-native

Habitat: wet or dry, sun, along roads, open fields

Range: throughout

Stan's Notes: A non-native plant introduced from Europe via Eurasia, Yellow Sweet Clover was once grown as a hay crop, but has escaped and now grows throughout Minnesota along roads and fields. This very fragrant plant smells like vanilla when its leaves or flowers are crushed. The genus name, *Melilotus*, is Greek for "honey," referring to its use as a nectar source for bees. Nearly identical to the White Sweet Clover (pg. 309), except for the flower color. It also blooms a couple of weeks earlier than White Sweet Clover. The rodenticide warfarin was developed from the chemical dicoumarin in sweet clover.

CLUSTER TYPE	FLOWER TYPE	LEAF TYPE	LEAF ATTACHMENT	FRUIT
Spike	**Irregular**	**Compound**	**Alternate**	**Pod**

COMMON MULLEIN
Verbascum thapsus

Family: Snapdragon (Scrophulariaceae)

Height: 2-6' (60-180 cm)

Flower: a club-like spike 1-2' (30-60 cm) long; of many, small, yellow flowers, ¾-1" (2-2.5 cm) wide, packed along the stalk, each flower has 5 petals and only open a few at a time, from the top down

Leaf: large basal leaves, 12-15" (30-37.5 cm) long, with thick covering of stiff hairs, velvety to touch; stalkless upper leaves (cauline) clasp the main stem at alternate intervals, leaves progressively smaller toward top of stalk

Bloom: summer, fall

Cycle/Origin: biennial, non-native

Habitat: dry, sun, fields, along roads

Range: throughout

Stan's Notes: A European import, this plant is known for its very soft, flannel-like leaves, hence its other common name, Flannel Plant. This biennial takes two years to reach maturity. The first year it grows as a low rosette of large, soft leaves; in the second, a tall flower stalk sprouts. It's said the Romans dipped its dried flower stalks in animal tallow to use as torches. Early settlers and Native Americans placed the soft woolly leaves in their footwear for warmth and comfort. Victorian women rubbed the leaves on their cheeks, slightly irritating their skin, to add a dash of blush. Its dried stems stand well into winter.

CLUSTER TYPE	FLOWER TYPE	LEAF TYPE	LEAF ATTACHMENT	LEAF ATTACHMENT	LEAF ATTACHMENT
Spike	Regular	Simple	Alternate	Basal	Clasping

CHECK LIST/INDEX   *Use the boxes to check wildflowers you've seen.*

☐ Alexanders, Golden 393
☐ Alfalfa 39
☐ Alumroot 77
☐ Alyssum, Hoary..............225
☐ Anemone, Canada..........231
☐ Anemone, Rue................217
☐ Anemone, Wood 221
☐ Arbutus, Trailing 243
☐ Arrowhead......................197
☐ Aster, Flat-topped 307
☐ Aster, Large-leaved 17
☐ Aster, New England........139
☐ Baneberry, Red................263
☐ Baneberry, White............265
☐ Bearberry 179
☐ Bedstraw, Northern 267
☐ Bellflower, Creeping 31
☐ Bellflower, Tall 19
☐ Bellwort, Large-flowered 345
☐ Bergamot, Wild 135
☐ Bindweed, Field 253
☐ Bindweed, Hedge 275
☐ Black-eyed Susan............359
☐ Blazing Star, Prairie 153
☐ Blazing Star, Rough 151
☐ Bloodroot......................239

☐ Bluebells, Virginia 21
☐ Blue-eyed Grass 9
☐ Boneset 277
☐ Bower, Virgin's................291
☐ Bunchberry 237
☐ Butter-and-eggs 389
☐ Buttercup, Aborted 63
☐ Buttercup, Swamp..........335
☐ Butterfly-weed 85
☐ Calla, Wild 271
☐ Campion, White 223
☐ Cardinal Flower..............175
☐ Catnip 285
☐ Cheeses 125
☐ Cherry, Ground 323
☐ Chickweed, Common 177
☐ Chicory 25
☐ Clover, Purple Prairie 137
☐ Clover, Red 163
☐ Clover, White 205
☐ Clover, White Prairie......261
☐ Clover, White Sweet 309
☐ Clover, Yellow Sweet 399
☐ Cohosh, Blue..................73
☐ Columbine 167
☐ Compass Plant................379

☐ Coneflower, Gray-headed 355
☐ Coneflower, Green-headed 361
☐ Coneflower, Purple 147
☐ Coneflower, Thin-leaved ..349
☐ Coralroot, Spotted..........159
☐ Corydalis, Pale...............115
☐ Cress, Winter..................357
☐ Cucumber, Bur 241
☐ Cucumber, Wild 303
☐ Culver's Root 311
☐ Cup Plant 381
☐ Daisy, Ox-eye.................255
☐ Dandelion, Common 343
☐ Dayflower, Asiatic 7
☐ Dock, Prairie 365
☐ Dogbane, Spreading 95
☐ Dutchman's Breeches......209
☐ Everlasting, Pearly 251
☐ Fireweed 121
☐ Fleabane, Daisy 99
☐ Forget-me-not 3
☐ Four-o'clock 91
☐ Gentian, Bottle................27
☐ Gentian, Fringed 45
☐ Gentian, Yellow 235
☐ Geranium, Wild 141
☐ Ginger, Wild 59

☐ Goat's Beard 353
☐ Goldenrod, Canada 391
☐ Goldenrod, Stiff..............383
☐ Goldenrod, Zigzag..........351
☐ Groundnut 61
☐ Gumweed 331
☐ Harebell 15
☐ Hawkweed, Canada 325
☐ Hawkweed, Orange..........79
☐ Heal-all 37
☐ Hemlock, Water 293
☐ Hemp, Indian 215
☐ Hepatica, Round-lobed 11
☐ Hepatica, Sharp-lobed......13
☐ Hyssop, Giant Blue 41
☐ Indigo, False 57
☐ Iris, Blue Flag 51
☐ Iris, Yellow Flag..............375
☐ Ivy, Ground 5
☐ Jack-in-the-pulpit 75
☐ Jewelweed 333
☐ Joe-pye Weed 119
☐ Knapweed, Spotted 133
☐ Labrador Tea 281
☐ Lady's Slipper, Pink 111
☐ Lady's Slipper, Showy 273
☐ Lady's Slipper, White......199

☐ Lady's Slipper, White......199
☐ Lady's Slipper, Yellow 363
☐ Laurel, Swamp 161
☐ Lead Plant 43
☐ Lily, Bluebead 213
☐ Lily, Prairie.....................87
☐ Lily, Turk's-cap................89
☐ Lily, White Trout 219
☐ Lily, White Water...........301
☐ Lily, Yellow Trout...........337
☐ Lily, Yellow Water 385
☐ Lily-of-the-Valley, False ..203
☐ Loosestrife, Purple..........155
☐ Lotus, American 397
☐ Lupine, Wild 53
☐ Marigold, Marsh 341
☐ Medick, Black 313
☐ Milkweed, Common 107
☐ Milkweed, Swamp..........173
☐ Milkweed, Whorled 245
☐ Motherwort 117
☐ Mullein, Common..........401
☐ Mustard, Garlic 259
☐ Nettle, Hedge 109
☐ Nightshade, Bittersweet..123
☐ Oats, Wild 327
☐ Onion, Prairie 105

☐ Orchid, Purple Fringed ..149
☐ Orchis, Showy...............131
☐ Paintbrush, Indian..........165
☐ Parsnip, Cow.................305
☐ Parsnip, Wild 369
☐ Pasqueflower 35
☐ Pea, Partridge 339
☐ Pennycress.....................249
☐ Phlox, Wild Blue 47
☐ Pickerelweed 55
☐ Pineapple-weed 65
☐ Pipsissewa 103
☐ Pitcher Plant 171
☐ Prickly Pear 367
☐ Primrose, Evening 395
☐ Puccoon, Hoary...............83
☐ Pussytoes 229
☐ Pyrola, Pink 113
☐ Queen Anne's Lace 297
☐ Rattlesnake Root 189
☐ Rocket, Dame's 127
☐ Rosemary, Bog...............181
☐ Rue, Early Meadow 283
☐ Rue, Tall Meadow 295
☐ Sarsaparilla, Wild 71
☐ Shooting Star.................129
☐ Smoke, Prairie...............157

☐ Snakeroot, Black 201
☐ Snakeroot, White 247
☐ Sneezeweed 347
☐ Solomon's Seal, False 299
☐ Solomon's Seal, Smooth ..67
☐ Spiderwort....................33
☐ Spring Beauty 191
☐ Spurge, Leafy.................315
☐ St. Johnswort, Common 329
☐ Star Flower 187
☐ Strawberry, Wild 207
☐ Sunflower, Common 387
☐ Sunflower, False 371
☐ Sunflower, Woodland 373
☐ Tansy, Common.............377
☐ Thimbleweed.................227
☐ Thimbleweed, Long-fruited257
☐ Thistle, Bull 169
☐ Thistle, Field 143
☐ Toadflax, Bastard 69
☐ Toothwort, Cut-leaved ..185
☐ Touch-me-not, Spotted 81
☐ Trefoil, Birds-foot............317
☐ Trillium, Large-flowered 289
☐ Trillium, Nodding 233
☐ Trillium, Snow................193
☐ Turtlehead 279

☐ Twinflower......................97
☐ Twisted-stalk, Rose 93
☐ Valerian, Common 269
☐ Vervain, Blue 49
☐ Vervain, Hoary 145
☐ Vetch, Crown.................101
☐ Violet, Bird's-foot 23
☐ Violet, Canada 211
☐ Violet, Downy Yellow 321
☐ Waterleaf, Virginia............29
☐ Wintergreen...................183
☐ Wood Sorrel, Yellow 319
☐ Yarrow, Common 287

GLOSSARY

Alternate: A type of leaf attachment where the leaves are singly and alternately attached along the stem, not paired or in whorls.

Annual: A plant that germinates, flowers and sets seed during a single growing season and returns the following year only from seed.

Anther: A part of the male flower that contains the pollen.

Axil: The angle formed between a stem and a leafstalk.

Axis: A point on the main stem from which lateral branches arise.

Basal: Leaves at the base of a plant, near the ground, usually grouped in a round rosette.

Bell flower: A single downward-hanging flower with petals fused together that form a bell-like shape.

Berry: A fleshy fruit containing one or many seeds (e.g., a grape or tomato).

Biennial: A plant that lives for only two years, and blooms in the second year.

Bract: A leaf-like structure usually found at the base of a flower, often appearing as a petal.

Bulb: A short, round, underground shoot used as a food storage system, common in the Lily family (e.g., onion).

Calyx: The name for the collective group of all of the sepals of a flower.

Cauline: Leaves that attach to the stem distinctly above the ground, as opposed to basal leaves that attach near the ground.

Clasping: A type of leaf attachment where the leaf base partly surrounds the plant's main stem at the point of attachment; the leaf grasps the stem without a leafstalk.

Cluster: A group or collection of flowers or leaves.

Composite flower: A collection of tiny flowers that appear as one large flower. Usually made up of ray and disk flowers, pertaining to members of the Aster family (e.g., common daisy).

Compound leaf: A single leaf composed of a central stalk and two or more leaflets.